We Died With
Our Boots Clean

We Died With Our Boots Clean

The Youngest Royal Marine Commando in WWII

KENNETH McALPINE

To my Amy

Author Kenneth McAlpine joined the Royal Marine Commandos at the age of seventeen and spent the war years fighting in France and Holland. After the war he became a wine merchant, writing articles for specialist publications on the subject. He lives in Bournemouth.

First published 2009

This edition published 2011

The History Press
The Mill, Brimscombe Port
Stroud, Gloucestershire, GL5 2QG
www.thehistorypress.co.uk

British Library Cataloguing in Publication Data.
A catalogue record for this book is available from the British Library.

ISBN 978 0 7524 6042 0

Printed in the EU for History Press.

'If you're not standing in more than two feet of water get them boots cleaned.'

Standard advice of all NCOs at all times

Contents

Introduction

This is the story about an infantry section of very young men cast in the dramatic role of private soldiers in a major war. The members of the section varied according to its manifold ups and downs; only Fred Waring remains constant in my memory from start to finish, though all are remembered in both face and voice. Ever since its fighting role came to an end I have read a great deal of military history, especially from the point of view of the other ranks. What on earth is 'other rank'? It is the only rank that can actually win you a war; the basic or private soldier is supreme in what he does in battle large or small, everything depends on him. All the same I rather think that during the fighting in Normandy – apart from our very best private soldiers – the German version did rather better than our own. To take a cricketing analogy, the Wehrmacht even after five years of war seemed on a level of excellence with the awesomely ruthless West Indian test match sides who ruled the cricketing world for almost fifteen years, terrorising all with their unending fast bowling bombardment and unassailable batsmen.

The German Army had been preparing much longer for war, was better trained, and its troops were brilliantly taught in the tactics of battle. They were significantly better equipped in every weapon, none more so than their armour, and they had access to large numbers of elite troops heavily motivated by fanatical Nazi ideology. The various SS formations – there were over 800,000 of them in the German Army – however morally deviant were superbly led at all levels and at times not far from invincible. The argument in the British Army hierarchy over whether more pro-saic units were detrimentally affected by extracting their better soldiers for elite infantry raged on after the war, though surely it might always have been possible to train up this vast majority into elite status themselves, why not? I used to wonder how we managed to emerge triumphant from the campaign, France through to Germany. I think Churchill said that the British were a martial but not a military race; there certainly appears not to have been much trouble taken in the form of intelligent military planning between the two great wars, and amongst our generals we quite definitely had no Marlborough or Wellington. There was Montgomery of course, self-publicist and apologist, forever excusing himself and bickering among his fellow Allied leaders. Further down the scale there were divisional generals of nervous disposition, full of anxi-ety to avoid any further Somme-like casualty lists that could be laid at their door, and failing to underpin the whole edifice were poor administration and second-rate basic training, Special Forces being a lonely exception. The result was that when war became largely attritional the really decent troops were overused to the point of exhaustion. In Normandy we got away with it thanks to a marvellous artillery service and the wonderful performance of the RAF in providing unending fighter bomber support – another form of artillery. Nearly 1,000 Marines were killed in the fighting from France to Germany in 1944–45, while three times that figure were wounded. Four members of 3 Section died in action at that time and several were wounded.

My friend Fred Waring was a cockney, born well within the sound of Bow Bells. This was important to him and added a lot to his joie de vivre, esprit de corps and general feeling of 'zut alors'! He was small, tough, and sceptical of authority, a working class lad with a fine sense of the ridiculous. I was tall, somewhat bemused and a public schoolboy. We were paired off under a system of 'two together', in the recognition that all infantry fighting is done by small groups of men working together in conditions of extreme intimacy where the better one gets on together the more successful the fighting and the better the chance of staying alive. We were initially tutored and lectured by a long serving soldier in the shape of Alistair McGonegal, a fierce and unsmiling character who would have put any number of pirate captains to flight at a single glance. When it was all over Fred made good money selling jellied ells at the end of Southend pier and on Saturdays outside his local football ground, while McGonegal disappeared back into the Scottish Highlands and became a ghillie, a stalker and a preserver of game for a surprised aristocracy.

Considering that they faced what has been referred to as the finest fighting army of the war and one of the greatest that the world has ever seen, I think that Fred, the two Alfs, Nutty, George and Bill from Bolton, not to mention the terrifying McGonegal, all of 3 Section did pretty well.

1945: Holland – a Taster

It was March, the weather had changed for the worse, a fierce wind blew from Siberia and a good deal of snow fell on 3 Section crouched by the roadside trying to brew tea in a disused biscuit tin. Archie Duff, five feet four inches tall on a good day, whose Dad ran a greasy spoon on the Great North Road, was in charge and not doing terribly well. Fred and I were guarding our backs. Without warning, some 20 German soldiers emerged from a small wood 50 yards away. We saw them first, the tea brewing operation was abandoned and after a brisk fire fight which we won thanks to the Section machine gun being handy, the enemy surrendered. There were a dozen survivors, their shoulder flashes showing them to be Hitler Youth SS who had an appalling reputation in Normandy where they had carried out atrocities, including the garrotting of Canadian paratrooper prisoners with their own parachute cords. We lined them up with their hands clasped behind their necks while Archie and I went forward to search them and collect their weapons. Fred stood to one side, his sub machine gun at the ready. As we worked along the line of prisoners, the German on the flank opposite Fred flipped a stick grenade from his boot and lobbed it just wide of Fred; it rolled into a ditch and exploded. Fred started shooting, sweeping along the line until his magazine was empty.

There was a long pause, a collective gasp from 3 Section, and an almost orgasmic groan. Fred's reply to the section was 'Up yours an all!' and he stamped off up the road to make the tea.

The next day was Fred's birthday and mine; small flakes of snow littered the ground and the wind continued blowing from the Russian Steppes. 3 Section had just been fighting their way through a small village vigorously defended by Dutch SS troops who fought with small ropes around their necks shaped into a gallows knot to remind them of their fate if captured by their fellow countrymen. One house remained to be searched before we could move on towards a brew of hot, inevitably awful tasting tea. Fred and I were detailed to do this undemanding job. We approached the steep steps of a smart detached house undamaged by the fighting. I waited below to cover Fred while he moved up ready to hammer the door in. He was on the top step where the door opened and out came a German general. We knew his rank because of his opening remark as he stood looking down at us, pistol in hand.

'I am a full general in the Wehrmacht and I wish to surrender to an officer of equal rank.'

'And I'm Adolph bleedin' Hitler, drop that pistol or I'll blow yer bleedin' head orf' replied Fred. The general retained his pistol.

'I am a full general in the Wehrmacht and I will not surrender to a private soldier, I will only surrender to an officer of equal rank.'

'Where am I going to find a full bleedin' general around here? Drop that bleedin' pistol and put yer 'ands up or I'll blow yer bleedin' head orf.'

'I repeat,' said the general 'I will only surrender to an officer of equal rank' and he continued to keep a firm grip on his weapon.

'If you don't drop that pistol and put yer ands above yer 'ead by the time I count to three, I'll blow yer bleedin' 'ead orf' said Fred, and he started to count. The full general had just got to 'I repeat I will only ...' when Fred shot him. As he fell down the steps, quite dead, Fred said 'Perhaps that will equal things up a bit.'

Just then Lieutenant Bird arrived. He was an amiable chap with a voice that reminded me of Stanley Holloway's character of the same name: 'his tonsils needed pruning.' 'What have you been up to now?' he asked Fred, who told him. 'Oh God,' said the Lieutenant, 'just think of all the paperwork. Get him buried quick.' We did so in a bed of what Archie Duff, a keen gardener, said were likely to be geraniums. Fred claimed the episode to be a moral victory. He was to have the chance of another moral victory that afternoon.

We were having a quiet smoke on the first floor of a small house in the next village, separated from the rest of the section who were busy searching houses on its far side, when a distinctly large German tank rumbled into the village and pulled up outside our temporary den. Without consultation Fred dropped a grenade down onto the tank. If he had waited 30 seconds he could have popped it neatly into the tank as its officer opened the hatch. Of course that might have blown up the tank and us with it, not that subsequent events took much of a turn for the better. The grenade bounced off the side of the tank and exploded in the doorway of the house. We raced across the room and shot through a small window onto the kitchen roof, from there onto the ground and thence via a cabbage patch, over a wall and into a bed of manure. The tank backed off a short distance and blew the house into small pieces. Fred reported that we had repulsed an attack by a heavy armoured vehicle. We are still waiting for the medal.

2

1930–1938: Early Days

I suppose I was about five when my parents promoted me from having a nursemaid to a full-blown nurse. Nurse James was certainly that and a good deal of sexual dawning emerged, at any rate on my side. She had a large welcoming lap and an enormous bosom which to my surprise and delight swayed free of any moorings excitingly to and fro. Above all, she was welcoming and warm, smelled deliciously of talcum powder and Knights Castile soap and creaked about the nursery in a mass of old fashioned leather accoutrements. She slept in the same room, taught me my prayers, hugged me a lot and made me feel very excited. I thought she was worth half a dozen mothers.

I enjoyed saying prayers and was encouraged to compose my own. I usually started off with, 'God bless Mummy and Daddy', and followed up with everyone I liked that I had come in contact with during the day. I finished with our four dogs but reversed the order promoting the dogs if father had shouted at me, or my older brother Ronald had thrown me into a pond. On a really difficult day under Nurse James' successor, I left everyone out except the dogs. 'God bless Taffy, Tinker, Puck and Sam, and make everyone else as nice as them' ran my main prayer that night.

Eventually some lucky chap snapped Nurse James up and married her, leaving me in the care of a thoroughly unpleasant woman called Nurse McGuffie, who confiscated my teddy bears and beat me using an ebony-backed hairbrush with fiercely unpleasant bristles. When she was finally dismissed, after I had complained about her through floods of tears, my mother asked 'Why didn't you tell me about her before?' She knew little of the fear imposed by an out and out bully.

However, worse followed in the form of another tyrant, Madame Dupont, who spoke little English and took me to watch French horror films. One particular example of the genre haunted me for years. It involved a multiple murder where the villain invited several guests to dinner and, when they were all seated, disappeared behind a curtain, threw a large switch and electrocuted all his guests who shot into the air with ghastly expressions of dismay and horror, before resuming their seats in a state of utter rigidity, quite dead. Their host then did peculiar things to the women and relieved the men of their wallets. For a very long time I wandered our house at night armed with a golf club and torch, too terrified to settle down. Father found me once and gave me quite a beating with a Malacca cane. It was small but hurt quite as much as the earlier hairbrush. It was an age before I dared complain about the awful Madame Dupont.

Occasionally I found some light relief with mother when she was free from sitting on almost every committee in the county palatine and I enjoyed our weekly visits to the cinema. One day, arriving home after seeing George Arliss in *The Iron Duke* and an exciting recruiting film for the RAF, which we sat through twice, we met a well dressed stranger coming down our main staircase.

'Good afternoon, Madam,' he said, 'the pipes are quite alright now.'

'Oh thank you' mother answered.

'I'm off on my holiday now, Madame' the man advised her and tapped a large suitcase. Mother wished him a pleasant holiday and he left by the front door with most of her jewellery.

On another occasion we stopped to give a lift to a rather distressed looking woman mother spotted by the roadside. Once in the car the woman produced a knife, pointed it at mother and kept saying 'drive on, drive on, don't stop!'

'I'm going to drive you home' Mother said, with splendid presence of mind. The woman thanked her and we pulled up outside a nearby police station where we all dashed in including the sad woman with the knife.

Despite all this palaver my next and final nurse was an absolute winner. Her brother held a first mate's ticket with the Cunard line and we went round lots of splendid ocean liners together as they arrived and sailed from Liverpool. Not least she showed me the delights of Edinburgh rock in all its six wonderful flavours, and that was well worth waiting for.

About that time I reached the advanced age of seven and was sent to a cheerful school held in the house and grounds of a former Lord Mayor of Liverpool where we were taught history from a book called *Our Island Story* and learnt that one English man was worth half a dozen French men and the same number of Scotsmen any day of the week, and we only lost the Battle of Hastings because the French cheated by feigning retreat, while the Scots did much the same at Bannockburn by digging unnatural hazards before the fight had even started.

Girls gave me a lot of trouble at this stage. I was almost the only boy in our road and was pestered by any number of little girls who invited me to their parties and offered to kiss me if I ate three slices of cake. I tried not to but I liked cake. A girl called Denise asked me to her party and reduced the going rate to two slices and eventually the embargo was removed entirely and I was kissed more or less non-stop.

Denise once said to me, 'If you show me yours, I'll show you mine' and when I asked her what she thought mine was, she said 'Your water spout of course.' I was on my way out to the garden to look for it when I met my older sister who explained this esoteric fact of life to me and ticked Denise off. Back at school, Rhoda

Hunter, whose father made pork pies on a rather large scale, used to gaze at me and twang her knicker elastic. I was known, unfairly, as the King of Sefton Park and while still only seven I was sent away to boarding school.

Whatever went wrong later at public school, the next five years spent among the Worcestershire hills in the care of a really good preparatory school, Abberley Hall, were splendid and I treasure the memory still. To be sent away from home to a boarding school at the age of seven is not an easy experience, but once I recovered from the initial shock and mild despair I felt content, positive and outgoing. Everything was straightforward and manageable, familiar, full of commonsense, strong routine, with no differentiation, sudden changes or mystery. It was not a home-from-home but it was admirably suited to its era and my needs at that time. I think the dormitories provided as good an insight into the general attitude as anything. No one saw any reason to spoil us with comfort, warmth, cosiness or style. It was not unkind nor unusual; it was the way things were in the 1930s.

The dormitory floors were bare boards but heavily polished, and there were marble washstands with chipped enamel jugs and bowls. There was a rota for boys to fetch water, often cold, seldom more than warm, for washing and to carry away the slops, which were poured into heavy buckets and emptied regularly down the sluice. Toothbrushes were made of bone, wood and bristle, and soap came in large carbolic blocks. There was no central heating and bedside drinking water could freeze on cold nights. We had chamber pots under the beds, which were sometimes used as curling stones, sent skilfully across the highly polished floors only to hit a cast iron bed leg and shatter, distributing the contents in all directions. The beds were of a model from ancient military barracks and hospitals of the First World War. We had two sheets, one red woollen blanket and a pillow, but we could supplement the blanket with another one brought from home should a cold spell threaten. Bedding was folded and stowed in ways prescribed and we made our beds after breakfast every day. We had to learn

and rigorously apply 'hospital corners', a complex fold and coun-
ter-fold procedure. All this was followed by dormitory inspections
with minus and plus points entered on a scoring card and all preceded by early morning cold baths.

Our evenings were punctuated by a strict sequence of events:
we had a time to say prayers, a time for Bible reading by rote from
the dormitory volume, spoonfuls of nourishing malt in the nurse's
surgery, Vaseline for chapped knees and wintergreen lotion for
bruises. We were allowed to play one gramophone record followed
by early lights out and a secretive reading of comics by torchlight
in our beds. Our daytime activities were quite different, being full
of variety and cheeriness. We played all manner of sport and games
– the Headmaster was an international cricketer and amateur foot-
baller – and we enjoyed weekly silent films and exciting lectures
given by men who had survived adventures with cannibals and
crocodiles.

In the grounds there was a very deep black lake where a famous
diver came to show off his craft. We all took turns to pump air to
him as he descended wearing an immensely heavy old-fashioned
diving suit. He disappeared for quite a long time and we had hopes
of an exciting climax when he suddenly came to the surface covered in a great cloud of bubbles and an abandoned overcoat. He
took off his great helmet and lit a small black cigar, puffing away
happily. After a few minutes we helped him replace his helmet and
down he went again omitting to throw away the cigar. He was
down quite some time before his frantic messages to bring him
to the surface were understood and acted upon. He burst to the
surface the cigar still between his teeth.

We had to suffer occasional beatings for undisciplined behaviour but there was nothing unfair about them as was the case later
at my public school. When I finally left the school there was an
exciting 'birds and bees' lecture from the Headmaster. It was quite
explicit and included the information that a man placed his 'thing'
inside a woman's 'place'. When asked what the 'place' was he said

it was a small hole. For some reason I enquired the size of the hole and received the reply 'quite small'.

'What if the man's 'thing' won't fit in the hole?' He laughed and he didn't often laugh.

'You needn't worry, you'll find it will cater for all sizes.' I felt relieved.

I left this splendid school with very considerable regret.

3

1938–1942:
One or Two Changes

For three years I was sent away to Repton, now a famous and splendid place in all respects but then a rather grim, disorganised public school in the North Midlands from where I eventually ran away to war. It wasn't a really bad school though it lacked a regularly attending headmaster, and its teaching staff were either embattled veterans of the Somme, Ypres and Paschendale, belching the remains of their ghastly gas experiences over the classroom, or they were young men away scoring double centuries while captaining their counties before dashing off to Oxford or Cambridge to complete their degrees. After that they would return in their Territorial Army uniforms and still further on they would reappear to show off their ever more splendid forms of military dress. One even came back to show us his tank. Sadly he was killed shortly after.

When I was sixteen I entered an essay competition sponsored by some august body with links to the school, an annual affair of no previous interest to me. The subject was 'Name your favourite historical character and discuss.' Everyone I mentioned it to had chosen Pasteur, Franklin Roosevelt or Leonardo da Vinci.

I decided on Bing Crosby. I gave as my reason that he had practically invented the American popular song, had a lovely deep purple sort of voice and made people laugh and be happy. My entry was rejected as being frivolous and that Crosby was without wide enough influence. When I said that 24 million people listened to his weekly radio show and 40 million worldwide to his Christmas broadcast (60 million when television came along), I was reluctantly allowed to go ahead. I persuaded a musical friend to write the notes of Bing's signature tune as my headline statement and I won first prize of a book token, which I sold on to my serious book reading sister and spent the money on a fine collection of Bing's early recordings, which kept me singing and whistling for ages.

Bernard Foulquies, or B.M. Foulquies de Mariabiault to give him his full name, was a close friend during my school years at Repton and with whom I shared the bottom two places in classes pertaining to all things scientific and mathematical. He was in school in England during the early part of the war – having been sent by his father to perfect his English – and though the war intervened he stayed put along with his father who was the owner of a family silk business left behind in Normandy and a friend of de Gaulle, a colonel in the Free French Army gathering in England at the time.

At school his teachers treated him as a dunce and ne'er do well and more or less wrote him off, not untypical of staff at that time. When football was arbitrarily abolished Bernard and I jointly protested, walking rather than running the races which replaced the sport carrying explicit banners of protest and creating whatever administrative mayhem we could.

It was not long after I absconded (of which more later) that Foulquies left too to become a Chasseur Alpine in the newly formed Free French Armoured Division. He became a Lieutenant fighting in Normandy and won the Croix de Guerre. I believe he commanded the first tank into Paris on 24 August 1944. I vividly recall trudging along a dusty road in Normandy one early August day that year and being herded away rather forcibly into a nearby ditch as an entire brigade of the Free French Armoured Division swept past in full panoply of war before coming to a halt quite close to us.

As we watched, pretty French girls jumped onto the tanks and threw garlands of flowers at the smiling tank crews. Not knowing that my best friend may have been in the leading tank and annoyed at being pushed into a ditch by military police, I hurled a large piece of earth and several bunches of dandelions onto the first vehicle in the line before they all roared away to liberate Paris. My friend swept down the Champs d'Elysees, over the Place de la Concorde before coming to a halt in front of the Palais de Justice where he took the surrender of some of the first Germans of the Paris garrison. After the war Bernard married the daughter of his commanding officer, ran his family's silk firm with distinction and both trained and raced horses from his own stables in Kentucky. Not bad going for a dunce!

I still have a happy memory of the visit of Geoffrey Fisher, the third former headmaster to become Archbishop of Canterbury and a lovely man with five sons who were my contemporaries at Repton and good friends. The *Sunday Pictorial* was unfairly attacking poor Fisher at the time over his salary and he chose his sermon in the school chapel to make a marvellously witty response. He was present at a reception at the Headmaster's house before attending the first 'School versus Old Boys' soccer match held since before the war, at which I was one of the goalkeepers. I am not proud of what I did prior to the reception, though it seemed a jolly jest at the time, when arriving early at the intended party I substituted the expensive luxury cigarettes called Passing Clouds which had been laid out on a special plate for the Archbishop's use with the cheapest cigarette imaginable, a real working man's 'gasper' called Woodbines. It was such fun to watch the Archbishop of all England light up his Woodbine and declare, 'I really enjoy a proper cigarette.' Later on he got his revenge at the football game when he approached my goal with two of his sons calling out, 'Hello, Kenneth how nice to see you again.' Delighted but distracted I turned towards the friendly greeting and the school in my temporary absence scored the winning goal.

I admit a certain amount of misbehaviour – or high spirits – at school but I always put body and soul into any activity I thought to be worthwhile. If we were about to play cricket and there was a jug or two of ale set ready in the visitors dressing room, I might help myself to see what it tasted like, but my bowling always benefited, being keener and faster following a good swig or two. I followed this routine at an away game with a famous, hitherto unbeatable school and their magazine praising my bowling declared it to be the fastest and fiercest seen on the ground for years. We easily won that game and the landlord's cat at a Public House close to the local station enjoyed a glass of brown ale with us on our return home. At soccer there was no beer, only lemons and cold tea, but we still did well against the several professional teams from nearby army camps.

The problem with japes of any kind was the certainty of the penalty. The inversion of a chamber pot on the spire of the assembly hall certainly attracted a severe one. The attitude of the school authority seemed to me to be a trifle negative and lacking in humour when judging these pranks, which after all, entailed a lot of hard work and a high degree of initiative. In fact the school sponsored punishments for wrongdoing on a grand scale. These were dredged up from historical routines relentlessly and cheerlessly enforced. Highly favoured were beatings with a cane, shoe or heavy leather slipper. Much of this had occurred at my preparatory school but there had been a sense of rough justice at that place. I found the present regime both painful and more significantly an embarrassment. At sixteen going on seventeen I was nearly twice the size and not that far off in intellect to my demon interlocutors and resented the implication that a good hard beating served all ills. I thought the better answer to my style of indiscretion would have been to make me a prefect.

I suggested this to the Headmaster in the middle of one beating but he turned me down.

I was once beaten for invading the housemaster's private apartment at 7am one morning to switch his radio through to the boys' recreation room at the far end of the building where I hoped to listen to Bing Crosby. We were forbidden our own radios and gramophones because a previous headmaster's wife had complained of their noise during an illness. Although many years had gone by, and the rest of the school were allowed to play their music to their hearts' content, with the present Headmaster living far away in a house of his own, our restrictions stayed in force and their contravention led to corporal punishment.

I also got into a lot of trouble because of a crush I conceived for one of the dormitory maids, a quite outstanding girl in every direction. I wrote her a poem detailing my love and desire, which if not perfect in rhyme and scansion, was certainly heartfelt. I addressed and left it on my pillow for her to find. However, the Headmaster's wife found it and told her husband, who got very excited and told me to report for punishment. I took the precaution of lining my behind with plenty of blotting paper and asked him why he considered my simple verses merited punishment. He said his wife had been very upset and I unwisely suggested he should write her a poem or two, so he increased the number of strokes with the cane from four to six.

I had been a keen member of the first eleven-cricket team and nothing short of a sensational goalkeeper, but our idiosyncratic Headmaster abolished football during the Easter term in favour of endless steeplechases and delayed the start of the cricket season to accommodate sprints and hurdle races. So I pushed off to become a schoolboy war hero. I was sixteen and six foot three inches and I decided to leave during an Officer Training Corps parade. The school had a unit replete with heavy boots, much brass to polish, webbing to Blanco and 1914 puttees to wind round our legs. We were constantly drilled by old company sergeant majors, veterans of many a scrap on behalf of Empire; their mantra of 'Chin in, chest out, neck erect' lives on in my dreams. The whole twice-weekly affair was not unlike the Royal Marines at the time I joined them shortly after.

I left the parade with my chin in and my chest well out and returned to my school house. I wrote a short note to my best friend and gathered together my belongings – a silver three-penny piece, two copper pennies, half a Mars bar and a cucumber. My mother, who thought it would come in handy with wartime sandwiches, had sent the cucumber to me, and it came in very useful almost at once because I met the Headmaster just outside the house. He wanted to know where I was going. I presented him with the cucumber, a gift to him from mother I explained. He looked very surprised but said he liked a good cucumber and would write to thank her; we moved on without further conversation.

It was not long after that that the governors dismissed the Headmaster for spending too much time away from the school looking after indigent boys clubs in London. What about the boys at his own school I wondered?

I had decided to head for Cambridge where I had a friend called Michael Dancy, who had just left school to go to Clare College. I felt fairly sure of my reception because we had been on a cycle tour the previous summer which had run into a spot of bother when a German bomber with one bomb left over after raiding Bristol almost dropped it on us as we climbed Porlock Hill near Minehead. The bomb fell not far in front and showered us with a good deal of West Country soil and stone.

I left the school grounds striding across the first eleven cricket pitch, climbed a fence, waded through a somnolent River Trent and buried my straw hat, complete with bright cricketing ribbon, deep beneath the soil on the far side. I was wearing an anonymous grey suit, mercifully a recent uniform replacement for black tails and stiff white butterfly collar. Far away I could see a long straight stretch of road, which I hoped would take me south, and I walked hopefully towards it.

A newly married couple in a tiny Austin Seven stopped for me and took me down into Leicestershire towards a further lift in a lorry full of hot tarmac, which brought me to Huntingdon where I ate my Mars bar and booked into the first hotel I saw. I explained to the pleasant woman owner what I was trying to do and she offered to put me up for the night, feed me and deliver me next day to my friend at Clare College, from whom she would collect my dinner and breakfast dues. She also sponged and pressed my suit, did my laundry and in the morning her husband telephoned Michael and drove me into Cambridge. When the adventure finally came to an end I wrote to thank them and a lot later on, during a short leave while in the neighbourhood, I went to see them.

I stayed a week with Michael. It was the time of the German Baedecker raids on cathedral cities and 'Lord Haw-Haw' (William Joyce) was broadcasting over Berlin radio, threatened that Cambridge would be next. I repaid some of my stay by fire watching at night on the roof complete with stirrup pump, a bicycle pump attached to a short length of hose before being plunged into a bucket of water in an effort to stifle incendiary bombs. Michael lent me some money and telephoned his brother on leave from the Scots Guards that I would be looking in on him at his home in East Sheen near Richmond. He also wrote to two wonderful maiden aunts who lived in Bath, with similar advice and finally to a farmer and his wife in Cornwall, with whom he had spent a family holiday, telling them to expect me.

A rather peppery RAF Squadron Leader gave me a lift into London in his green MG, not helped by my hopeless map reading, there being few if any signposts at that time. I spent the night at the Alexandra Hotel next to what used to be St George's Hospital at Hyde Park Corner. Bombs flattened the hotel the next night. I went to Richmond and met Michael's fierce Scots Guards brother who made it clear he thought I should return to school, but gave me half a crown and a large pork pie. I left London by the western route.

On my way out of London I stopped at an important road junction to ask directions at a large garage. A lovely girl serving petrol helped me and drew a splendid diagram, well ahead of anything the AA could have managed, and I walked slowly in the midday sun along the old Bath Road. As I passed a bus stop a bright red bus pulled up and out jumped the pretty girl from the garage in a surprisingly clean pinafore, green jersey and heavy Wellington boots. She gave me a resounding kiss on the cheek, a hug, a large ham sandwich and a ten shilling note. 'With love from the girls at the garage,' she said. She walked across the road and I watched her as she got on a bus. I think she was the first girl to kiss me since Denise Nixon in my early nursery days.

I stayed that night in a hotel near Reading and apologised to the owner for my not very clean appearance. 'That's alright,' he said, 'you speak nicely,' and he sent me up a plate of sandwiches. It was not until 10pm the next evening that I reached Bath to find I had lost the address of Michael's aunts, but there they were waiting for me at the station.

'We came last night,' they told me, 'but felt we had to try again tonight.' They put me up in what I suspect was their own bedroom, and sent me on my way the next morning with a fine picnic lunch. I travelled down to Cornwall by train to Padstow, found Michael's farm and spent a rather aimless week doing odd jobs. At the weekend I went into town and was arrested by the Padstow police as an escaped prisoner of war.

We know you speak good English,' the two policemen told me, 'but you have a large white patch in the seat of your trousers.' This was a wartime repair in the 'make-do-and-mend' campaign of the school matron, and indeed looked similar to those applied to prisoner of war clothing. It took a long time to explain this and I was interviewed for nearly an hour at the police station. My innocence was finally established after a complicated phone call to my father in Wolverhampton, who sent me some money by telegraph to help my homecoming and settle my debt to the farmer. I didn't go back to school but rather joined the Wolverhampton Home Guard.

I learned later that the Headmaster had hired a private detective to capture me at a nearby mainline station and another one at a London terminus, but after two days they had gone home.

The Wolverhampton Home Guard was an energetic military unit advised and trained by the South Staffordshire Regiment. We held ingenious exercises in the town centre where we defended Molyneux, the famous football ground, from a German glider borne assault. We recaptured the main trolleybus depot after an enemy parachute landing and by mistake routed a battalion of Dutch troops stationed in the town, before setting fire to the town hall. On Sundays I manned a Vickers machine gun kept in the living room of a neighbour – the local officer for customs and excise – which we were allowed to fire on some waste ground at Courtauld's local factory. The lads from Warmington-on-Sea had nothing on us.

While this was happening I found a job at the local labour exchange in charge of the call-up section and had the satisfaction of calling up the former assistant headmaster of my old school who had recently taken over the headship of a nearby establishment, although his appeal against my decision was upheld. During the whole time I spent establishing myself I was desperate to find a recruiting office, the nearest being in Birmingham. I told them I wanted to be a fighter pilot but failed their colour vision test. The army wouldn't take me until I was 18 and I failed the Royal Navy's colour test but they said they would accept me as a colour-blind stoker or a Royal Marine. I asked them what function a Royal Marine fulfilled and they said jack-of-all trades and, after passing an esoteric round peg in a square hole test, I signed up for the Marines and awaited their call to arms.

When the great day arrived I was met at the station by a Chief Petty Officer who told me I was to take charge of a group of young lads from Birmingham and escort them safely to Portsmouth. They were my first experience of the working classes and I was certainly the first product of an English public school they had seen and they ragged me unmercifully to the point where, changing trains near Portsmouth and watching a gang of convicts chained together on their way to the Isle of Wight, I felt they might have had the best deal. I found it difficult to survive our first night together in barracks, especially when they made me an apple pie bed with a very large lump of coal in it. However this seemed so typical of what went on at boarding school it made me burst out laughing and they laughed too. We quite quickly became pals and in various permutations continued that way for the next four years.

The Royal Marines are an interesting regiment always referred to as 'the Corps'. Apart from the French Foreign Legion I can't think of a military formation that comes close to them for refined disciplined endeavour. As commando soldiers they are unique. All commandos these days are Marines and all Marines are commando-trained. When I joined, the regiment had failed to build on its fine light infantry traditions being, in the words of a former colonel, 'lost in a whirlpool of indecision regarding their proper function.' Why, for example did they man so many big guns of the fleet? Were there not skilled sailors to do this? Of course there were. What a waste of fighting infantry, only partly remedied by the wartime emergence of the Commandos, which was the invention of the British Army not the Marines.

They did a very good basic training however, with a dash of *Dad's Army* thrown in. Plenty to endure, much to laugh at. We drilled to a point of absurd excellence, we scrubbed and 'squee-gied', folded our kit and blankets into amazing shapes and patterns and paraded at 6am each day in semi-darkness. After the initial shock, we stopped resenting the relentless drills and became fit, enthusiastic and thoroughly expert.

For years, because of my height, thousands of men, from Portsmouth to Dortmund, from Inverness to Hook of Holland, knew where to form up and dress ranks smartly. I was number one on parade wherever I went. It was the one thing I did really well. Along the way we suffered the pangs and joys of indoctrination. We were taught our real aim in life, which was to always excel the Guards regiments in everything we did. The Germans may have been our intended enemy but the Guards would do in the meantime and spit and polish to peacetime requirements reigned supreme. We lavishly spread polish on our boots, and set them on fire before furiously boning away with our toothbrush handles. Other occupations including hurling grenades, sticking pineapple bombs on the side of broken down tanks and firing, dismantling and reassembling a Lewis gun, then defunct even in the Home Guard.

These early proceedings were brought to a close by a 25-mile night march round the Solent and back to barracks. I brought up the rear carrying a red lantern. We were met at the gates by a small band detachment composed of a large drum, a fife, two bugles and a tenor saxophone. The musicians struck up 'Colonel Bogey' and 'A life on the Ocean Wave', and we donned our gas masks and doubled at some speed into barracks.

Nor was our general knowledge neglected. One miserable wet day our squad sergeant organised a quiz and recreation period. We only got as far as the first question, 'Name the wartime British Prime Minister?' After a long pause, someone called Arthur, pronounced 'Arfur,' said he knew the name of the German chap in charge, and Fred suggested a Mr Hatlee, which one of the several Bills who drove dustbin lorries around London, said proudly, 'Erbert Morrison is our MP, my mum does his washing'.

None of this pleased the sergeant who declared he had never seen so many ignoramuses in one place before. Fred Sealey from Liverpool, who had delivered telegrams before the war on a small motorbike, asked what an ignoramus was and when the reply came, 'Numbskull!' Ginger, the undertaker's apprentice inquired what a numbskull was. What struck me as being so nice about it all was the consensus remark when it was finally revealed that the name we were looking for was Winston Churchill.

'Oh! We thought he was too important to be Prime Minister'.

On the way to a well-earned lunch Fred said, 'Ere, who's the bloke who said an army marches on its stomick?'

'Napoleon?' I suggested.

'Who?' said Fred.

We didn't do too badly. I read somewhere that six per cent of Sherborne School when recently interviewed for a national magazine thought that turnips grew on trees. Keep in mind that our pay at this time was only 14s or 70p a week.

My squad sergeant told me I had managed a 91 per cent record throughout these six months and had been recommended for commission training. I can't remember on what specific grounds I turned this splendid offer down, though I did feel that with the fighting round Stalingrad turning against the Germans, the war might disappear before I could become involved, so perhaps I didn't want to waste time on further lengthy training. At any rate, the Portsmouth depot adjutant called me a bloody fool and that I was missing a chance of a lifetime and sent me away for a week to think it over.

I confirmed my decision to the adjutant who told me he had nothing more to say to me and I was drafted away to a naval gunnery course. Luckily this did not last more than a few hours before I dropped a large shell weighting some 20lbs on my foot and was withdrawn from the course for a week of 'excused boots' and put on light duties peeling several thousand potatoes. I also volunteered for commando service and while waiting for this to percolate through the system I volunteered for landing-craft training which was to be based in an old co-op jam factory in Lowestoft.

During my week of suspended animation my foot refused to repair itself and I had a further need to report sick. The period from my recruitment days to my last week in the Corps to report sick was regarded with deep suspicion. In barracks you had to apply for permission from the company sergeant major by 7am – permission only, mark you. An intensive grilling ensued and if you emerged unscathed, off you went to the sick bay. Here, heavy resistance was encountered from the corporal assistant and you could easily be diagnosed as a malingerer. The few who got through to the medical officer were subjected to scorn and disbelief in full measure and, unless you actually died during the cursory examination, you found yourself back on the parade ground where the squad ser-geant noted your name as a potential troublemaker. I once felt wretched while on night picket duty outside the barracks. In the morning I reported sick at the nearby infirmary, but they refused to examine me and I was returned to duty. After another unpleas-ant night during which I coughed up blood, I tried again. I was reluctantly taken in overnight but discharged once more without diagnosis or treatment. On the way out I took my temperature and found it high but this time, having to come back yet again, I brought my blood along in my tea mug.

'Is this your blood?' The corporal attendant wanted to know.

'I got some of it from Count Dracula but most of it is mine.' At this point the medical officer emerged.

'Don't try to be funny,' he said 'and next time bring any blood to me personally.' I was in hospital for two months with pneumonia and met Ginger. He had been helping his father in his undertaking business when he decided it was all a bit quiet and volunteered for the Marines. We shared a small ward of four or five beds in a depressing naval hospital first opened when Napoleon was in his prime, which had not changed much since. Ginger entertained me with his cheerily detailed accounts of funeral adventures. These included the near burial of his local town mayor while there was still a good deal of life left in him; an occasion when the hearse was stopped for speeding; and the day the police, searching for a suspected murderer, stopped Ginger who was driving the hearse for a routine search and found a body in the boot. He once asked me how tall I was and when I told him he said, 'If you were a dead body and had lived in a top flat we'd have to break both your legs at the knees to get you down in the lift!'

On my return to duty again I had a further need to report sick. I was helping a very nice though not terribly bright chap called Trefor Evans load a machine gun and 25,000 rounds of ammuni-tion – which was contained in a heavy metal box – onto a lorry. Trefor managed to collapse the gun and its tripod, which, together with the ammunition, fell to the ground, bouncing on its way across my back and shoulders and onto Trefor's feet. He couldn't walk and I couldn't stand. Following negotiations, during which several peace treaties in Bosnia could have been signed, we were allowed to report sick.

The medical officer, a large man with a face like a hippopotamus about to submerge, awarded Trefor three days of light duties but when I told him I thought I had broken a bone in my back he referred me to a framed motto on the wall behind him. It read, 'It's all in the mind and the heart.'

'There is no such thing as a back injury at your age' he declared 'and I recommend you to reflect on my motto, especially that bit about the heart, that's where your problem lies.'

We departed to find the squad sergeant outside, who asked what the medical officer had to say to us.

'He told me I'd got a badly bruised foot,' Trefor said proudly, 'and Lofty 'e's got a broken heart.'

On active service any attempt to report sick was almost a court martial offence even if you were out of the line resting. And yet once real fighting got underway attitudes changes completely and you could hardly move for fear of being examined and bandaged. Medical officers and their assistants cared for the wounded under fire, winning medals for bravery by the dozen, but once the shells and bullets eased off medical routines reverted to the disinterested lack of attention one was used to.

It came as a surprise therefore when, filtering through the barrack gates en route to the railway station and my demobilisation, I heard the MO call out, 'Stop that man sergeant, he's got an infectious looking rash.' Half an hour later I was in an ambulance on my way to an isolation unit on Hayling Island, expertly assessed as having contracted German measles which was known to be disastrous to unborn babies, there being no inoculation against it in those days and it being so infectious that a simple sneeze could spread the germs.

Entirely fit and well once more, the landing-craft volunteers made their way to Lowestoft and joined the training squadron there. There were twelve craft. They had flat bottoms and weighed 11 tons with a top speed of 8 knots or 10 miles an hour. We sailed to and fro around the coast in foul weather, combating seasickness by chewing stale bread. Twice we called in at Dover and became involved in a heavy bombardment by the giant German naval guns at Cap Gris Nez 22 miles away. We were shepherded here and there by destroyers hurtling about, sounding their klaxon horns and ringing bells to warn their crews of sudden heartstopping high speed changes of direction. Sometimes they stopped dead in the water like a skier slewing expertly round to come to a halt in the snow. We watched great plumes of water where enormous shells fell amongst the assembled shipping, along with whizzing chunks of random metal often clanging alongside. It was our first taste of action; we only called in for lunch.

At Slapton Sands in Devon we practised with a US infantry battalion and knocked off for lunch at opposite ends of the beach. Several hundred seagulls weren't wrong when they decided to eat with the GIs.

We were billeted at Dartmouth in the Naval College on filthy mattresses and endured fleas and lice and itched away with scabies. However, it was there I met Fred, which was a marvellous piece of luck. On Sundays we had formal church parades, which only catered for Protestants and Catholics; any other denomination could fall out and make their way to an appropriate place of worship in the town. The morning could then be spent in the Salvation Army canteen enjoying baked beans and the *News of the World*, but first you had to survive cross-examination from the officer running the parade. Fred and I agreed to be Plymouth Brethren.

'What do you understand about Plymouth Brethren?' the officer asked Fred.

'They were brothers from Plymouth who sailed on the *Mayflower*' was Fred's surprising reply.

'Oh,' said the parade commander,' I suppose you sailed on the *Mayflower* too?'

'No sir,' said Fred 'but I was on the waiting list.' We were allowed to be Plymouth Brethren for the rest of our stay.

About then my chit came through to report for commando training and my landing-craft friends carried on a year or so later to land the Newfoundland Regiment on the Normandy beaches and eventually they went to Burma. There is a memorial to them on the Hard at Itchenor near Chichester and to the 32 members lost in a storm on the passage back to England from France. Storm warnings came too late for them.

The US troops were shortly to become part of a bloody and accident-prone affair codenamed Operation *Tiger* when Slapton Sands and an extensive surrounding area was chosen as a rehearsal area for the American D-Day landing on Utah beach in Normandy, which it closely resembled. Many miles around the south coast of England became a strictly enforced military zone; 750 families totalling 300 people from 180 farms and villages were evacuated in the space of three weeks. The contents of churches – crucifixes, silver crosses and plate – were removed to safety and an exact simulation of the intended invasion area took place. Live ammunition was used, shells were fired and bombs dropped in major quantities and as exact a schedule as possible was prepared in advance of D-Day.

The first part of the rehearsal went well and it all seemed worth while until nine German E-boats slipped out of Cherbourg Harbour in the dark and evaded the naval screen set up to protect the 25,000 American troops and their supplies all heading for Slapton Sands. E-Boats were 100 feet long carried two large torpedoes, were always painted black because they mainly operated at night and were capable of speeding along at over 40 miles an hour. They torpedoed and sank two large landing ships weighing 5000 tons each and with a top speed of barely 12 miles an hour, severely damaged a third and apart from losses of equipment on a grand scale, well over 700 American soldiers were killed – rather more than were killed on Utah beach proper on D-Day.

For reasons said at the time to be connected with security, no official mention was made of this sad event for ten years. A complete cover up was engineered; the recovered bodies were simply hidden away and were not given any form of recognition either through burial or on their hometown war memorials. Finally on 3 May 1984 a comprehensive admission arrived via nationwide television coverage in America which revealed everything, including all errors and omissions, of which the most important was that the marauding E-boats had actually been spotted by UK radar while still in harbour but their movements were only followed up for a very short distance thereafter. I don't know if our newfound friends on the beach at Slapton Sands survived or not.

4

1942–1943

'I want you always to give 100 per cent and then without hesitation immediately another 30 per cent.'
Standard commando requirement, oft repeated by inspecting generals

Commando basic training took place on the Clan Cameron's estate at Achnacarry, which had been requisitioned by the British Army. It was not far from Ben Nevis; the nearest station or halt was Spean Bridge some seven miles from camp. The experience remains one of the most amazing and exhilarating of my life. It started with an eleven-hour train journey followed by a final seven-mile speed march across Rannoch Moor.

I think Baden Powell introduced speed marching as part of Boy Scout training. Perhaps its origins were during the war in South Africa when messages had to be carried over vast distances during the siege of Mafeking. Telegraph posts were used as markers and messengers would run 20 paces and walk five arriving in no time at all at an average speed of nearly five miles an hour. Our commando speed marches, alternate running with walking across rough country carrying rifle, pack and ammunition, would cover 9 miles in 90 minutes, though when that was accomplished we often had to run a further mile non-stop.

It was a rough camp; some of us spent our six weeks in tents while others were allocated Nissen huts. There was no heating or electricity and only very cold water coming to us direct from surrounding snow-covered mountains. The commandant's opening address explained what he wanted from us. There would be no unreasonable demands but they were to be set high. He expected us to give 100 per cent and then, without hesitation, an extra 30 per cent. We were never to fail in this and in addition we were to acquire ideals and the spirit to live up to them. In this we must prove ourselves without question.

If the camp was rough the training was more so. Nothing that came later, apart from the fear factor of close quarter fighting, surpassed the trials and torments we endured at Achnacarry. The failure rate was about a third. On the other hand nothing matched our moment of triumph when to the sound of pipes we were awarded our green berets, the ordeals of the brutal course mastered.

Most of the work was physical. We paraded at 6am each morning, were issued salt pills and for half an hour did loosening-up exercises that would have tested a gorilla to its absolute limit. Then came breakfast accompanied by bagpipes. We speed marched everywhere, swung on ropes over rivers in full spate burdened by pack and rifle, often crashing down into the water. We were pushed through long and complex assault courses, attacked by our instructors with live ammunition and stun grenades. As we crawled along a muddy stream beneath a bridge, our instructors emptied containers of cattle blood over us. They then jumped down from the bridge and drove us back into another group of instructors hurling more stun grenades at us.

Whenever training seemed to have reached its climax and there was a lull and we relaxed, an even worse catastrophe would present itself. We once started up Ben Nevis in a blizzard with a pound of meat and one match apiece for our lunch. I could only singe my meat, for any kindling scraped out of the snow was too damp to provide a flame. In fact nobody managed to do better before their matches fizzled out and they then attacked it raw.

Halfway up the mountain the clouds came down and the assault was called off. When we reached the bottom the instructors speed marched us to another mountain without cloud and without food. We had been told on no account were we to resort to any form of communal cooking. On another similar exercise we were given two matches each to cook the meat but once again we all failed except Fred who managed to secrete a phial of lighter fluid. I think the record speed of wind blowing off the top of Ben Nevis is 150 miles per hour, which would explain why only Fred got anywhere close to having roast beef for his dinner that day.

We did a lot of rock climbing in heavy boots more suited to marching and even less suited to abseiling down a very steep cliff. I had climbed up behind the padre who used many exciting swear words which were new to me. Our instructors rigged a tightrope from the top of the cliff to the ground at an incline of 100 feet or so. They hauled up a machine gun and slid down the rope, arms outstretched like a gliding bird. Landing happily then called for volunteers to do the same. One of the instructors looked at me and I thought I was done for, but by an enormous stroke of good luck somebody else actually stepped forward, climbed the cliff and came flying down the rope carrying the gun and emerged alive at the bottom. He was awarded his green beret at once.

For variety we were taught to cook, mostly rats and small birds, though sometimes we snared a rabbit. Everything we cooked had to be eaten. We fought each other with commando daggers and learned the Mexican methods of knife fighting, under arm rather than over arm. We fought with bayonets and, in unarmed combat, learned how to kill someone in seven seconds. An instructor demonstrated, using me as the victim. I vividly remember falling to the ground with a grey film across my eyes and in great pain. I was told I would have had two seconds to live. After that we practised on each other.

We trained on all kinds of weapons, often blindfolded as we dismantled and then reassembled them. We came to realise that the German weapon equivalents were far better than ours. I still remember four stoppages on our light machine gun and the same number on the German version.

Further delights included 'milling' – standing toe to toe for three minutes of non-stop punching and not allowed to step backwards. If you were knocked down you got up and toed the line again. Three minutes may not sound long but it felt like an eternity, especially if the opponent was a stone heavier.

The final two days of the course produced a storm of activity. An epic march of 30 miles in full gear (a pack alone weighed 40lbs), up and down steep hills ended at dusk. As we fell out we were attacked yet again by our instructors with their stun grenades and forced in our turn to attack them, though we only had thunder flashes. Finally we had to dig in for the night still fighting off our persistent instructors until dawn, when we speed marched back to camp and, without breakfast, went straight into our final day which thankfully ended in the award of our green berets. However, yet more was to come.

On our way back to camp we halted and were told to attack and capture a small island 200 yards offshore in the centre of a distinctly large loch. We had to row ourselves in large old fashioned whaling boats with five oars on each side. Progress was slow and perilous because the instructors came along too in their own boats spraying the water ahead of us with live machine-gun fire. On landing we climbed a small hill in heavy muddy conditions and when we reached the top found moving targets arranged some 30 yards away which we had to shoot at. Entirely out of breathe we had to fire five rapid aimed shots at these targets and keep shooting until we achieved a score of five out of five on each target. Then back to camp we rowed, the instructors giving a repeat performance and, after four giant corned beef sandwiches, into bed only to find our blankets had been soaked in cold water. We were roughly awakened at 4am and told to fall-in complete with pack, rifle and ammunition and undertake a competitive march with a company of US Rangers who were also in camp. The winners would be whoever could march furthest in four hours. We won easily because, as always, we speed marched and the Americans merely marched.

The taking of prisoners was dealt with during a lecture – in fact the only specific lecture I can recall. I don't think many course instructors, though skilled in all aspects of commando training, had experienced actual combat. I have no idea why this was so but their views differed, often widely, from those held at commando level. The lecturer stated that prisoners must be treated as laid down by the Hague Convention, all fair, clean and above board, without exception. This was backed up at senior officer level in fighting units, but the reality was quite different down amongst the grass roots. I think the general feeling was that anyone wanting to surrender was making an offer that needed close examination before any acceptance was made. From the point of view of the soldier wanting to surrender it was a question of luck and timing. There were too many exceptions for any form of routine decision to be made or enforced.

Casual snipers were hated and couldn't expect to hang around shooting and then decide to surrender when they thought the time was right; it never was for them. Unofficial training with the Commando told us to make sure that enemy wounded who might in any way be able to take hostile action once they had been passed by, were definitely to be killed. No one forgave or forgot the behaviour of wounded enemy soldiers who, given a drink of water or other help, then shot their Good Samaritan helpers. The random killing of prisoners was not countenanced but neither was the slightest liberty rashly taken by any intending prisoner.

This lecture really did mark the end of our basic commando training and after breakfast we marched to the initial accompaniment of the camp pipe band, the seven miles to Spean Bridge station and a troop train heading south which took us to Wales via Shrewsbury railway station, where my much loved Aunt Violet appeared with a large cylindrical tin full of superb Eccles cakes. How she knew I might be there remains a mystery unless she met every passing troop train on a speculative basis. Sadly, she died shortly thereafter, a lovely lady and a very considerable pastry cook.

We found ourselves in a camp high up in the Welsh mountains and when Christmas arrived we were given the day off. We decided to try and eat four Christmas dinners to settle a substantial bet we had with a man of spectacular physique and enormous appetite called Dai Griffiths who was a member of the permanent camp staff. Dai held the record for Christmas dinners, having eaten two the previous year, but we felt that as there were two cook houses in the camp this had been made easy for him. Our battle plan was simple, we speed marched the six miles into Towyn the nearest town and, by special prior arrangement with the Queen's Hotel staff, we sat down to eat at 11am and quickly polished off two lunches. For digestive purposes we adjourned to the Salvation Army canteen for a nice cup of tea, read the newspapers and speed marched the six miles back to camp where, with only mild indigestion we joined the cookhouse queues on either side of the parade ground. Our third Christmas dinner went down well and in reasonably high spirits we staggered into cookhouse number two just as it was preparing to close. We were admitted and sat down before what appeared to be an unassailable mountain of food. Just then two unpleasant looking military policemen came through the door.

'Now then, what have we here?' they enquired. 'We saw you in Towyn this morning stuffing yourselves at the Queen's Hotel, we then saw you at number one cook house just now and here you are still gorging away. Eating more than one lunch in camp is forbidden; two is a serious offence, let alone four. What's the matter with you? You must have got worms. Report to your orderly room first thing tomorrow for punishment.' With that they disappeared into the kitchen!

We duly reported to the orderly room and the duty officer said 'When I did my rounds the other day weren't you the men complaining that you didn't get enough to eat?' We had to admit that we had complained. 'Well, you've overdone it this time' he said.

The punishment was four days confined to camp – one for each dinner. We were told we had been guilty of sloth, greed and gluttony. Fred pointed out that sloth hardly applied because we had worked hard in pursuit of an aim, but unfortunately he explained what the aim was, so sloth was deleted and we were awarded an extra two days confinement for gambling. Nor did we win the bet; Dai refused to pay up on the technicality that we never attempted the Christmas pudding.

As we prepared to leave Wales I received a note from my mother.

Your letter from Wales has just come (Monday breakfast) and I am in process of wrapping up a cake I made for you yesterday. I will send it in a tin as the materials out of which cakes are made are rare and precious, but so also are tins. If there is a Post Office in your wilds could you post it back to me sometime? I enclose string and label inside, to make it easy. You do not mention if you received the £1.00 I sent to your former address in the wilds of Scotland.
Love Mother

In Wales I had my first romance, with a bonny ATS girl called Megan who wore a daring perfume called Californian Poppy. I always knew where she was even when well out of sight thanks to Californian Poppy, which she sprayed heavily over her letters writing the initials S.W.A.L.K. on the back of the envelope and adding below in brackets the message 'sealed with a loving kiss'. To reach Megan on my evenings off I had to walk seven miles along a rough railway track from the camp to Barmouth where there was a cafe with a view out to sea and a juke box with a Bing Crosby recording of 'My Bonny Lies Over The Ocean' on one side and 'You Are My Sunshine', Churchill's favourite wartime song, on the reverse.

Connecting Barmouth to all points south was a bridge where we shared a rather chaste kiss and another one at the other end of the bridge on the way back. I used to arrive in a smart pair of brogue shoes, which, thanks to the railway track and wartime repairs, soon lost their soles, and I had to fill the gap with a rolled up section of the *News of the World*. At the end of three weeks of walking along the Barmouth railway line the shoes gave way entirely and I threw them out to sea from the end of the pier.

We moved camp every two or three weeks at this time. In a way it was exciting to think of all the girls one could meet but unsettling too if you met one you wanted to see again and again. My newfound commando friends enjoyed the mobility and variety – their attitude was more aggressively extravert than mine – at least that was how they were keen to portray themselves.

Girls were judged through the key word 'passionate'. All their girls brimmed over with and simply oozed passion. Whereas my new friends mostly met their girls at a local dance, in pubs or on the street corner, I preferred a more organised approach and, where possible, I would contact a local camp, ask for the women's commanding officer and state my case. With luck I would be granted an interview with one of their girls and with more good fortune we would then spend two or three weeks of happy off-duty moments together. The choice was between the Air Force (WAAF), the Army (ATS) and the Navy (WRNS) or WRENS. I haven't forgotten the Woman's Land Army with their handsome Stetson hats and bright green jerseys, but they were hard to find on their lonely farms.

I remember the WRENS being most sort after though this was as much to do with their pretty legs in black stockings as anything. My favourite WREN was a Welsh girl called Gwen, with dimples on her knees who, against every regulation, wore high heels when she came out with me which helped to adjust our discrepancy in height. Her commanding officer gave her a tremendous ticking off, telling her that 'High heels have sexual overtones and must be avoided in wartime.'

Later on Bill Taylor came along. Bill had been apprenticed to his father who was a blacksmith. He was large, handsome, amiable and slow of intellect. He had contacted several magazines catering for young female readers and had built up quite a pen pal following, though he had seldom managed a reply. Perhaps 20 girls were writing to him in assorted coloured envelopes swarming with esoteric initials and drenched in exotic scents. Bill appealed for help. Together with a friend from our headquarters who controlled a typewriter and a supply of paper, I agreed to manage Bill's business – which it was rapidly becoming. We introduced a system of standard replies, including a couple of holding ones which told his correspondents he had received their letter and was longing to write back but he was too busy training to kill Germans to reply for a week or so. For some reason this gave him a tremendous boost and soon 50 girls were busy writing. Later on, when we were on active service, all his mail got forwarded and Bill had his own special mailbag, which came to him courtesy of the field post office. Eventually we had so many complaints from the authorities that mail was having to be diverted to cope with Bill's 200 letters a week, we had to stop. We arranged for Bill to be taken prisoner. He wasn't pleased but we allowed him to keep six of the most passionate correspondents, but he had to reply under his own steam. My favourite wartime letter found in one of James Agate's wonderful series of autobiographies, the *Egos* was one from an unknown private soldier in the First World War: 'Dear Mabel, I am not spending any money on women or beer. I am sending it all to you. So let me fight this bloody war in peace!'

We left Wales at the double, speed marching much of the way to Deal on the south coast. Here we resumed landing-craft training. There being no mountains we were kept busy with various jolly activities; one was to see how far we could march before our boots wore out, accompanied by a small lorry full of nails, spare boots and soles. I suppose this rather depended on the state of the boots to start with, but our boots were deemed in urgent need of repair well past Sheffield and, after an emergency stop for footwear first aid, back we came. A small part of the unit marched wearily on almost to the Scottish border before their boots wore out. They all returned by train.

Another idea was to tell us we had 48 hours to get to Aberdeen and back, a round trip of 1300 miles from the south coast, twice involving the crossing of two major rivers. However, we were not allowed to use public transport or to borrow or steal any vehicle. Given these restrictions, with private petrol being scarce and service vehicles not travelling far from base, this exercise gave us major problems, but it was accomplished with several hours to spare.

While we were at Deal I met Sergeant Major Bullock. We had been sent there to be smartened up and for our rifles to be attented to by the depot armoury. Months of living rough had put us in need of some cosmetic attention. Bullock was a large, red-faced man with a handlebar moustache of impressive size. He looked like an unsuccessful boxer of many years largely failed endeavour and had a voice that could shatter glass at 200 yards. His behaviour was bellicose, verging on malevolent. He was a straightforward bully, and after a fortnight of suffering his mean spirited treatment I was alarmed to be called to his office one otherwise pleasant sunny morning.

He glared at me from behind his moustache and produced an imposing document from his desk tied with a smart pink ribbon. 'I have your report here,' he shouted at me, 'It's a disgusting thing.' He held it away from him as if it contained several unpleasant diseases. 'I'm going to read it out loud so you'll know what other people think of you, and it gives me no pleasure to do so,' he added, warming to his task. 'You're lazy, idle and slothful, with marked criminal tendencies. You're a useless soldier and every unit you're sent to is glad to see the back of you. Now,' he shouted, thoroughly enjoying himself 'what do you say to that little lot?'

'Well,' I said, glancing over his shoulder, 'my name is not McFarland.'

'Wha'cha mean? Your name's not McFarland?'

'Well, it's not.'

'What is it then? It's down here in black and white as McFarland.' I showed him my pay book, which he examined, in great detail. 'Are you quite sure this is your proper name?'

'Yes, Sergeant Major, I've been called McAlpine since I was born, never McFarland 'till now.'

'Don't trifle with me, son' he roared loud enough to quell a dozen mutinies. 'Just you go and double round the parade ground and then you can go and get yer 'air cut. You need to lose 'arf a stone.'

We moved on from Deal to a former holiday camp at Bracklesham Bay in Sussex where the main dining hall and kitchens were still clearly marked in red and white paint 'Lancastrians' and 'Yorkists'. Why this was so wasn't officially explained, but someone who had actually stayed there said there had been quite a lot of partisan feeling stirred up by the camp staff with campers divided into 'Yorkists' and 'Lancastrians' and encouraged to throw bread rolls at each other twice daily. We were plagued twice by a visiting German Messerschmitt 110 which also caused trouble at lunchtime, dropping two bombs the first time and machine-gunning the camp the second. Flying splinters injured several of us and on the second occasion I went back to my hut to rescue a framed and signed photograph of Bing Crosby while Fred, who was next door, tried to do the same for Mae West who sadly was badly smashed up. The duty officer from the safety of a nearby ditch told us we would be reported for disobeying orders, endangering lives and goodness knows what other nonsense. At the orderly office proceedings the next day, which lasted nearly an hour and only ended when the air-raid sirens sounded again, we were severely ticked off.

By happy chance I met my elder brother nearby. He was twelve years older than me and practical jokes were his great love. To this day I feel relief when opening a door and not finding a deluge of water descending on me from a bucket above. He once gave me an interesting toy called a 'seebackroscope' which was an abbreviated telescope in shape which when placed to the eye would reveal everything going on behind as you walked along, in my case my brother hurling a bucket of water over me. When I withdrew the 'seebackroscope' from my eye I was left with a large black ring round it. His best trick, though not original, was quite dramatic. He would stop at a letterbox and peering down the slit carry on a sympathetic conversation with an imaginary person trapped in its depths.

'Now my little man,' my brother would say, 'I want you to be brave and cheerful and above all don't panic, the fire brigade is on its way.' Quite a large crowd would soon gather round and with a final injunction to the little man to hold fast, my brother quietly drifted away.

When war broke out my brother lived in Liverpool and at once hitched a lift to London in order to join the Scots Guards. Arriving at Chelsea barracks he joined a long line of young men being formed up in order of height by a Sergeant Major, who asked him his height. On being told 'five feet nine inches' he placed his hand on my brother's shoulder and said, 'You, and all to your left, left turn, King's Liverpool Regiment, everyone else stand fast Scots Guards!' An hour later my brother was on a lorry on his way back to Liverpool. He died in India en route to Burma where he is buried in Madras Military Cemetery plot 8, row A, Grave 17. I was at home on leave the day the War Office telegram was delivered by a young man on a small motorcycle. Father stopped cutting the grass and slowly read the telegram saying 'Give the messenger boy a shilling, I must go in and tell your mother.'

Letters kept arriving from my dead brother for several weeks.

In the home hierarchy Father was our chairman and chief executive with at least two seats on the family board, though Mother was called in from time to time as an expert adviser. My two brothers added a nihilistic touch to events, while my sister and I came along as minor postscripts. Father was well over six feet tall and handsome, with a profound bass-baritone voice that could be heard four floors up from the bottom of a lift shaft. His merest conversational whisper became a bellow. He was rather a severe sort of chap but mellowed over the years, producing fine touches of surprisingly gentle irony.

He was born in 1883 and while still in his twenties he became Professor of English at the University of Omsk in Siberia. He lived opposite an Imperial vodka factory and next door to Rasputin in his native village close to Omsk. He was the only Englishman to have met and known Rasputin – whom he liked – and was also the only Englishman to have lived in the Russian capital through both revolutions in 1906 and 1917. On his return he was recruited by British military intelligence and sent back to Russia. My father worked closely with the Russian Prime Minister Kerensky, visiting the battle fronts to see and report on the grim conditions of the peasant soldiers who shared one rifle between four, had one meal a day and no winter clothing. Later he infiltrated the Cheka – the Bolshevik secret police – arranged the assassination of its chief figure and conspired in two attempts to kill Lenin. He was seized during the Bolsheviks' revenge sackings of the British embassy building in August 1918 and imprisoned in the impregnable fortress of St Peter and St Paul from where no prisoner had ever escaped. Conditions were grim, overcrowding was so serious that men were often taken out and shot simply to make room for others. Twenty prisoners were herded together in a cell so small there was only one foot of standing room per man; they all had to stand up together and to lie down together on the cold bare floor. In one corner was a latrine which everyone to keep as far away from as possible, and there was one small sink and an iron bedstead fixed to the floor, which was allocated to the personal and confidential valet to the late Tsar of Russia.

Food was hard to come by; prisoners were fed twice weekly with bread and soup which consisted of hot water a few small bits of cabbage and tiny stinking fishlike creatures floating about. Exercise consisted of a ten-minute spell in the dull evil smelling corridor. Inside the cells insect life ran riot. It is impossible to say how long my father endured this awful place but several weeks later word was passed through that everyone was to be released except McAlpine who was to be shot. In early October he along with his batman George Stone escaped. How this was managed I don't know because he tended to be secretive about the whole affair, though referring once to a collapse of the building forming part of the cell block through which they made their way. Perhaps some form of outside assistance helped engineer the escape. I remember father saying that George Stone promised him free meals for life at his family's restaurant if they managed to get free. I certainly ate free of charge several times against the original promise. The Stone's family restaurant in Soho was featured in the *Good Food Guide* until the 1970s.

At all events they made their way to refuge in the heart of the capital and joined several of their fellow adventurers in time to take part in the rescue from Bolshevik hands of the Romanian government's national treasure which had been looted in course of invasion by Russia and taken to Moscow. This consisted of an enormous amount of currency valued at the time at £4,000,000 together with a trove of royal jewels. Again in this story details are scarce, but they rescued it all from secure Moscow vaults, transferring the jewels and currency from their steel cases into ordinary wicker baskets for disguise and trundling everything on sledges through the mob-infested streets to the station. They arrived 20 minutes before the train was due to leave for Romania and stacked everything in two railway trucks attached to a special carriage. A good deal of bribery must have been involved. At any rate off they went, perhaps six secret agents in all, travelling in course of their journey lasting nine days through no fewer than seven active battle areas, often indiscriminatingly shot at and enduring frequent searches of the train before arriving late one evening in the Romanian capital to be welcomed by the Minister of Foreign Affairs, the Railway Minister, and half an hour later the Romanian Prime Minister arrived too. In recognition of his part my father was invited to Bucharest at the end of the war to a public investiture and Queen Marie awarded him a splendid decoration, as also earlier had Karensky.

My father also had an adventurous life after the war, including an attempted return to visit Russia on his seventieth birthday when they refused to admit him. He became a big man in business before losing all his money in the futures market. He died in his ninetieth year while watching a Clint Eastwood film.

5

1944: D-Day

A battle is mostly to do with random pieces of flying metal and its awful effect on young men.

Haste to the Battle by J.L. Moulton

As spring turned to summer it became obvious that plans for invading Europe were not only underway, they were very close to completion. Equally apparent was that they would involve us in the main assault on what was already being referred to as D-Day. So, in early June 1944 I was holed-up in a small tent in a wood alongside the one furlong marker at Goodwood racecourse. Fred and I were swatting away flies while busily employed repairing the main latrine, we were singing along to one of the collection of Bing Crosby records contained in my spare kitbag played on an old wind-up gramophone.

A bugle sounded and we were all summoned to man the roadside and cheer a passing general who had been giving a pep talk nearby. Fred and I were well behind the others and, seeing an approaching cavalcade, we stood fast on our own at a bend in the road and as a group of three jeeps drew level, we waved our berets in the air and gave three rather ragged cheers. We clearly saw Field Marshal Montgomery in the centre jeep and were very surprised when they slowed down and he threw two packets of cigarettes at us. He called out something about having a 'crack at Jerry' and then he was gone.

The cigarettes were called Martins of Piccadilly and were a notorious wartime smoke, the ash curling rapidly up its paper with much snap, crackle and pop, and the cigarette was often set ablaze. We weren't too impressed by the great man's gift but we lit up. As we did so several more jeeps buzzed into view and, throwing our Martins 'firecrackers' away, we sprang to attention once more. The convoy stopped right in front of us and a four star US general wearing a pearl handled revolver and looking more like Roy Rogers than General Patton – who we thought he was – leaned over.

'You men smoke?'

'Yes sir.' The general waved to a military policeman wearing long white gloves and as the small procession pulled away a package flew through the air and landed at our feet – 200 Lucky Strike.

'Blimey' said Fred, 'we're in the wrong flippin' army.'

D-Day arrived after plenty of last minute delay and postponement spent in a completely concealed camp on Southampton waterside. We embarked the afternoon before in our small unarmed craft and sailed at dawn after an enormous meal of sausages and dehydrated potato – most of which went overboard during the night and early morning into a rough, grey sea.

Visibility was limited it was hard to see any great distance in the rain and thick mist. This dramatically interfered with a detachment of landing craft that also had to contend with a faulty compass. After sailing to and fro for what seemed an eternity they saw through the impenetrable fog a gleam of light and a stretch of beach. They turned inshore and headed for the beach where they landed some 200 assault troops who all struggled ankle-deep in shingle until, without opposition of any kind, they reached the esplanade where they found an old man leaning against the railings smoking a pipe.

'You're out early,' he said as he bent down to pat his dog 'another exercise is it?'

'Not exactly, where are we?'

'This is Brighton' said the old man. 'Where are you heading for?'

'Normandy, it's D-Day.'

'Ah, well. I can help you there' said their guide confidently, 'Normandy is that way' and he pointed out to sea. 'It's back the way you've come.'

The rest of us, seasick, cramped and uncomfortable, tossed, rolled and corkscrewed on our way. The fog had cleared and away to the east we saw a massive bunch of shipping apparently held in a queue behind several other large vessels flying the Stars and Stripes. We were told they were refrigerator ships carrying ice cream. Alongside us was a command ship, a large landing craft flying from its mast not only a White Ensign but also an enormous pair of *directoire* knickers. The colonel who was standing nearby murmured respectfully, 'They belong to a duchess, so I'm told.' We sailed on.

At about 8am we turned for the shore. The weather was dull and grey with steady drizzle and the heavy swell of the sea stopped just short of compelling further seasickness. Our stretch of beach seemed reasonably quiet but first we had to negotiate scores of underwater beach obstacles. These were large iron stakes referred to as 'Rommel's asparagus', festooned with explosive charges. There were two schools of thought as to how this problem could be tackled. Some thought it best to wait for a high tide which would cover the obstacles, while the opposite point of view advocated landing at low tide and avoiding them altogether. We had expected to land at low tide and were dreading the long time we would have to be under fire from the beach defences before we could reach them. While we were still two miles from shore this plan was changed and we came to a stop wallowing in the rough sea until the tide turned. In theory, therefore, we landed at high tide but in practice the tide was not fully in, the obstacles were much larger than we thought and for a long time we found avoiding them almost impossible. The sea became more turbulent and there was a wretchedly strong, indeed vicious tidal stream running parallel to the beach, which swept men away as they tried to swim, and drowned them in their absurdly heavy equipment. Some of the landing craft that struck the beach obstacles were blown up and sunk 100–200 yards away from the beach. Our craft hit an obstacle, got hung up and was left wallowing alongside it without power. Those that hit the beach had their own problems apart from the tidal rip, when all along the esplanade the enemy opened fire, at some points not much more than 100 yards away. Bullets hissed and spat along the surface of the water, but worst of all was the damage caused by a positive deluge of heavy mortar bombs. Most craft still stuck on the beach obstacles simply vanished under this bombardment. Our craft shook itself free from its obstacle and, out of control, rolled those of us who had survived onto the shore. Others waded to the beach from their damaged craft while a few just disappeared as they jumped off their stranded craft into six feet of water.

There was little help from the much-publicised naval bombardment, which on our beach we rated a failure. Enemy machine-gun fire continued nonstop with endless ricocheting from the armoured sides of the many tank landing craft where a major dispute broke out between three commandos rescued from their sinking craft and the lieutenant commanding the much larger landing craft which rescued them on its way to the beach. This vessel was hit by a mortar bomb and, without reaching the shore, promptly went astern and out of danger. One commando drew his pistol and held it to the naval officer's head and threatened to shoot him unless he changed his mind at once. He did and in they went again.

The beach we were trying to land on was not a long stretch of shingle but a large cove. It was sandy, strewn with obstacles and had two large rocks as well as an esplanade. Into the rocks had been inserted a German medium size field gun on one side and a smaller but deadly captured French quick-firing gun on the other. They were sited to enfilade the immediate offshore area. They now joined in the battle concentrating on the landing craft and a few intrepid tanks crowding onto the beach, which was now partially clear of the tide. Rescue came in the form of a brave action by the survivors of several adjacent landing craft, including Fred who I had last seen disappearing beneath an extremely large wave but who now reappeared to take the lead in the attack on the guns on the far end of the beach. There was a chaotic scramble up the rock sheltering the quick firing gun, and two satchels of explosives were dropped through the emplacement's aperture. Away went the gun and its crew up in the air, nearly killing us all.

After a frantic struggle sliding down the rock face, a group of us more or less recognisable once more as 3 Section, ran and finally crawled, not without a good deal of miscalculation, up to the larger gun and sprayed it internally with the contents of several sub machine-gun magazines. Ricochets wounded two of our number, but the gun never fired again.

The beach area was crowded with reinforcements milling around, enemy mortar and machine-gun fire remained intense and what was worse, accurate. Our own small mortars replied using smoke bombs, which were a blessing and meant that the Germans were forced to fire blind to a large extent. Tanks coming onto the beach, also blindly, became bogged down in the shingle and some were set on fire by enemy shelling. One tank ran over a group of wounded men but paid no attention. An officer nearby managed to blow off one of its tracks with a hand held anti-tank grenade, which brought it to a standstill. Mortar bombs continued to crash down and our section of beach was a jumble of abandoned equipment, wounded and dead men. The noise was deafening and unending.

Apart from our model of landing craft there were also converted tank landing craft, much bigger at 100 tons or so, and they carried up to a couple of field guns, cruising up and down the shoreline blasting away at pill-boxes and targets close to the beach and in turn making themselves simple targets. Sometimes they sank themselves in shallow water so close to an enemy battery that their gunners could not depress their weapons low enough to hit them.

After the landings some of the landing-craft crews stayed on unloading stores and ammunition from dawn to dusk in appalling weather that sank many vessels. They had no regular rations and for quite a long time were bombarded by land-based artillery and the Luftwaffe. They also had to collect up vast loads of what were thought to have been safely rendered landmines and dump them out to sea. If the mines exploded, and they often did, they sank the craft and killed the unfortunate crew. Here is the advertisement that appeared for many years in the Royal Marines journal, *The Globe and Laurel*:

601 LCM Flotilla Remembrance Service

The annual 601 LCM Remembrance Service will take place at the Memorial Seat on the Hard at Itchenor, on the 6th June to remember all Royal Marine landing-craft crews lost in Normandy and especially the 32 members of 601 LCM Flotilla lost in a storm on passage back to England.

The routine will be the same as always: gather in *The Ship* afterwards, followed by a trip around the harbour in the Harbour Master's launch.

There were about 10,000 marines employed during the Normandy landings and the landing-craft crews deserved to be remembered as well as anyone else.

Exciting additions to the weaponry were floating or DD tanks, the initials standing for 'Donald Duck'. These were 38-ton Sherman tanks whese engine power could be transferred from the tracks to twin propellers and by erecting high canvas screens all round they could float, just. Once on shore, power was returned to the tracks and the screen was jettisoned. On D-Day the sea was so rough that many DD tanks scheduled to land ahead of the infantry and to be launched four miles out could not be launched until within 700 yards of the beach or not far off half a mile away. The waves came up so high the crews had to climb out of their tanks and hold the canvas screens up by hand. It was a terrible way to land – awash with water, seasick, wearing their life belts and Davies escape apparatus. They went so slowly they were often run down by the many landing craft about. Other DDs plunged in from three miles out in a very rough sea, dropped their canvas screen on the beach and opened fire. The tide then came in rapidly and waves swamped their engine, so the crews then took to their dinghies which when hit by machine-gun fire sank, obliging them to swim. When or if they reached dry land again they lay on the beach soaking wet and exhausted. An awful lot of DD tanks never reached the shore; they sank like stones in the English Channel along with their crews.

Swapping experiences sometime later with survivors of an armoured yeomanry regiment they told how they had lost 27 out of the 29 tanks launched in rough seas some three miles out while their sister regiment had watched eight of their tanks sink between ship and shore. On the other hand not far away but sheltered by an abutting headland a similarly equipped unit had landed with 21 of their 25 tanks intact and given valuable support with their guns to the assaulting infantry. We wondered if senior officers involved in the planning of these operations with their unfair and dispropor-tionate odds against success ever became involved personally with these ghastly tanks where death by drowning was almost as likely as death by battle. These dangerously adapted tanks were highly approved of by Montgomery. It was a ridiculous strategic concept and tactically pointless because of the huge risks involved and the comparative ease of landing tanks right up to the beach on special-ist mass-produced tank landing craft.

At last someone discovered an exit from the beach free from small arms fire and we staggered away from what appeared to be the start of an official assembly area. Moving forward we encoun-tered heavy rifle fire from a trench behind the esplanade and this forced us to think again while we hid in confusion beneath the sea wall. We managed to advance our Bren gun team ahead and wide of the enemy position and it fired non-stop, magazine after magazine, forcing German heads down, just about giving us time to clamber up and over the sea wall. We charged at only moderate speed, weighed down by equipment and soaking wet clothes, to the other side of the road, firing our rifles from the hip as we went. Our machine gun stopped shooting and as we almost reached the enemy trench they stopped firing as well, throwing their rifles away and with hands in the air shouted and yelled, 'Kamerad, kamerad' at us. It was too late; they'd had their chance, they should have given up when we were much further away, we were too full of collective fear and frenzy to feel pacific. None of them survived; they were all shot or bayoneted.

We also had to contend with a woman sniper shooting at us from a tree that had been skilfully constructed to accommodate her, two specialist sniper rifles, and 200 rounds of ammunition. She didn't survive either. Another sniper fired at us from amongst the bells at the top of a church tower. Our bullets made a weird noise ricocheting from bass to tenor bell and back down the scale again. We couldn't get rid of him and no one fancied climbing a spindly ladder up a loft so we called up a small multiple firing anti-aircraft gun to blow away both the tower and the sniper. Others carried out the assault on the remaining strong points on or near the esplanade and we were given a break.

The seafront road and the parallel one behind it had been strongly fortified by the Germans. The sea wall was covered in barbed wire and there were several trenches running along this road while the parallel road inland had inset concrete machine-gun positions. All lateral roads were blocked; the windows and doors of all the buildings were bricked up and there were connecting underground passages. We enlisted the help of a naval bombardment to break into this formidable strong point but the storm of heavy shells entirely missed their target and flew inland. A passing tank from the Royal Marine Armoured Support Regiment opened fire and offered the promise of a breakthrough but ran out of ammunition. Another that blew up on a minefield replaced it. Further efforts involved yet another tank and anti-tank gun, which were also put out of action by mines and enemy fire.

A bitter close combat fight ensued. Our Lance Corporal medical orderly who was dressing a man's wounds was hit in the leg but continued his work when a second bullet struck him in the shoulder, but he did not seek cover and was killed by a third shot. We could not break into these fortified houses during the whole of what remained of D-Day.

We did have one major surprise at the end of the day. We discovered that the defending garrison had built permanent underground living accommodation for their women folk, actually joined up with or adjacent to their fighting position. Some of them had been there possibly for several years; even children had been there before the invasion.

The beach where we had landed was a terrible sight by nightfall when we started on some clearing up; bodies lay on their own or in small groups often torn apart, some were pulled well up on the beach while others drifted in and out along with the tide. There were burnt out tanks and landing craft, abandoned stores, tins of food and every kind of debris scattered everywhere. French civilians and their children scavenged among the havoc. No one seemed very surprised at anything they saw. We buried perhaps 100 bodies, some of them our friends, in the abandoned gardens of former strong points beyond the beach. We hung their hard won green berets on roughly-assembled crosses over our comrades and later a service was held and the French people brought flowers along. This temporary burial ground was later removed to a permanent sight at Bayeux.

As I walked along the beach I watched the Army's heavy lifting gear start to release the stranded and disabled landing craft helpless athwart the iron stakes that had trapped them both before and after landing. This was dangerous work because their explosive charges were often still in place.

Without food or a hot drink since early morning we set to in a brave attempt at a brew-up. We used a cut down biscuit tin as a kettle and we placed this on a surface of sand and pebbles on which we poured diesel fuel and set it alight. Teabags would have come in handy if they had been invented. Our tea tended to taste of smoke and diesel but was more than welcome.

We were warned to expect an armoured counter attack and we moved a mile or so inland to some rising ground and dug ourselves in. At night anywhere near the beach area the Luftwaffe had a go at us and thousands of ships of every size let rip with all their available weapons, from heavy anti-aircraft guns to handheld machine guns. The illuminated sky easily beat Blackpool and the noise and accompanying firework display was sensational, but it was all pointless and very expensive. No one as far as I know ever hit anything and it is a depressing fact that what goes up must come down; in our case an awful lot of random metal from exploding shells and bullets which fell down on top of us causing casualties and severe loss of sleep.

D-Day and the next two days cost the Commando well over 200 casualties with many killed and the assaulting landing-craft crews suffered on a similar scale. One Commando came ashore in sixteen of the smallest partially-armoured craft, each holding 30 men. They were landed, without casualties but twelve of the sixteen were destroyed on their way back to their depot ship, killing the three-man crews. The support craft – which were not unlike tubby launches or motor boats and were heavily armed with a miscellany of weapons – actually closed the beaches ahead of everyone else including the attacking infantry, as they had done in Italy and were to do again with almost total casualties at Walcheren Island in November. There is a nearby D-Day memorial stone to our Commando, which carries the injunction '*Souviens Toi*', 'Remember'. In front of the memorial is a dramatic cube sculpture made out of the compacted debris of war with the caption 'This is not a work of art. This is a work of war. 1944–1994. Never again.' The sculptor Dominque Colas presented it.

Looking beyond my own personal experience of D-Day, our enemy missed a simple opportunity to prevent the landing of several thousand Allied troops forced to use the inadequate landing craft that some of us invaded from. These craft held about 70 men;

they were made of wood and were totally without armoured protection. Passage in them was cramped and uncomfortable, so much so we preferred to take our chance on deck amid the rain-storms and very cold northerly winds. In order to land we had to tiptoe down two slender ramps each some 20 feet high which swayed to and fro from the bow of our craft; it was like trying to rush down a crowded escalator complete with people struggling to pass. When the craft beached these insecure ramps often threw people off into the water, a crazy gangway system, which doubled our peril, acute as it already was. If the German machine-gunners had fired more freely and intensively at us staggering down our wretched ramps they could have swept our wooden craft and mown down the helpless men inside trying to get out. The thin wooden hulls would never have kept out bullets and the preva-lence of the several thousand gallons of high octane petrol stacked up just behind the bridge of each craft could easily have burst into uncontrollable flames. Luckily one's enemy is not always as intel-ligent as he might be.

6

1944: Post D-Day

Having finally vanquished the enemy strong point overlooking the D-Day promenade, which had held us up during the first two days of the invasion, we reassembled to discover that the Commando was down to the point at which only half of our number was left. We moved a mile or two inland to take over some primitive defensive position protecting the beach areas from the parachute regiment of whose 6th Airborne Division we were now a part. Our mission was to defend the beaches against counter attack and protect the emerging build up taking place behind Caen ten miles inland. The enemy still held positions on the coast nearby and an armoured thrust in their support was considered a danger. If all this has sounded simple routine much looked forward to, it definitely wasn't. D-Day had been the most dreadful experience, quite traumatic in fact. Still, there we were and in one not dissimilar form or another there we were still mostly together arriving in Germany eleven months later, laughing a good deal not really properly fed and shockingly underpaid. The Canadians with whom we fought in Holland earned four times the amount we did and the Americans no less than eight times as much. This extraordinary disparity was confirmed by my two brothers who served with both the Canadians and the Americans.

To begin with our toehold positions in France consisted simply of freshly dug narrow slit trenches, which had to be rebuilt into some degree of permanence. Our situation was a mixture of marshland and open fields, no grim *bocage* country as yet. The nearest enemy were 400 yards away in a concrete strong point. Later on when we moved to Troan they were only 150 yards away and on one occasion an officer came round to pay us only to find the Germans were much closer at 80 yards. This proximity meant that normal speech was impossible and laughter was at a premium.

We were close to the village of Sallanelles where some civilians had defiantly stayed put in their houses and our medical officer in his off duty moments cared for their sick and injured. We had very little hope of a cooked meal to ease the unending boredom of composite tinned rations because no lorry dared travel up to the front line along small roads several inches deep in dust, which when churned up invited shell fire.

Part of our daily existence was enduring mortar bombardments or 'stonks' that landed without warning. Apart from the initial hiccup they were mostly inaudible in flight and their sudden arrival was nerve wracking. If they caught us out in the open and according to the ground they struck, their flying splinters could cause depressingly high casualties, nor was it pleasant when sheltering in the cellar of a house or cottage to have it suddenly blown to pieces over your head. Occasionally the enemy who blasted away with groups of 20 bombs a time would fit a siren which made them shriek and wail before landing with their usual thunderous crash. That really was a terrifying experience. Some of the bombs hurled at us weighed as much as 75lbs, though most rather less at 5 or 10lbs. Whether we attacked or defended, we would come up against a storm of mortar fire onto already prepared zones of fire. There were flying splinters everywhere.

Of course we had mortars too, and we had in Dusty Miller a splendid virtuoso in their use, but we seldom benefited from their support en masse as did our enemy, who used multi-barrelled projectors on track-mounted vehicles which appeared all over the place without warning and sent over much concentrated destruction. We feared and detested mortar fire even more than minefields and their frighteningly fast-firing machine guns.

I have used the words fear and terrifying rather often, but advisedly so because that was mostly how we felt, confronted by such a devastating arsenal of superior weaponry. Quicker firing, heavier weight of fire, better reliability and greater ability to spray a battlefield with all-encompassing destruction, the Germans had fabulous weapons from tank to pistol.

Once the Sergeant Major came running into our forward position shouting, 'Enemy tanks are coming our way, they're Tigers, dig for your lives,' before disappearing fast to the rear and safety. Fred and I dug up most of northern France in no time at all but alongside us, smoking his pipe and declining to dig, was Bill from Bolton.

'Them's not Tiger tanks, them's ours, yer silly buggers. Fetch out yer mugs and we'll tap' em for a brew of tea, they've stopped moving.' Bill was right; the Sergeant Major had a point though. The Tiger was the most feared tank of all. It wasn't quite true to say its gun was the length of a telegraph pole but it fired an enormous shell, was well protected by its armour and weighed 54 tons. A few days after D-Day these tanks had caught forward elements of a nearby commando alone in their slit trenches and literally buried them in the ground.

Our only weapon to try and combat their fearsome tank was called a PIAT (Projector Infantry Anti-Tank), a quite hopeless antidote. This was a sort of vague update on a medieval crossbow. It was spring-loaded and after infinite persuasion fired a 2.5lb shell. In the early models its large tail fin flew straight back at the gunner on explosion and gave him a lifelong 'tattoo' on his forehead. It had two loading positions, lying down, worth a double hernia, and standing up for a quadruple one, plus a bullet in the head from a sniper because the exercise, if away from cover, took so long. The gunner had to get close to a tank to be effective and it needed to be a very small, thinly armoured one. The distance had to be about 30 yards, the gunner had to be carefully positioned and the shell fired to avoid it glancing off the tank and, because it all took so long, he needed a decent life insurance policy. I fired our PIAT several times and frequently carted its bombs around into and out of action and I can affirm that it was a rubbish weapon, useful only for house breaking and blowing up bunkers. I believe several VCs were won using a PIAT, mostly posthumously. It was that kind of weapon.

In contrast the Germans had a fine handheld infantry antitank weapon called the Panzerfaust or 'armoured fist'. This was very effective in Normandy where Allied tanks could be approached at close range amongst hedgerow country. It was a one-shot weapon discarded after firing and weighed 10lbs against the PIAT's 30lbs and its high explosive charge was able to penetrate a Sherman tank's armour at 80 yards.

That German tanks were more powerful was obvious, but what really caused us alarm were the personal weapons in everyday use by infantry, which were not just marginally but very much better than our own. Even our rifles, though adequate, were not as good. We were using the 1914–1918 model until early 1943 when we moved on to a 'utility' version. Our pistols were less well balanced and harder to control on firing, our sub machine guns were ludicrously inferior, the Sten gun didn't even have a safety catch and was dangerous to use. As a design the German Army had turned it down before the war.

The main infantry battle weapon was the light machine gun, and in our case the Bren gun was nowhere near as effective in spraying the battlefield – its prime purpose – as the German machine guns known collectively as Spandaus. A Spandau's 1200 rounds a minute, with its terrifying whiplash, rasping sound, was seriously demoralising to fight against. In comparison our Bren could only manage 500 rounds a minute and a reassuring chugging noise. It was a good weapon but not really good enough. Our main hand grenade dated from 1917 and was very heavy to throw. The German 'Potato Masher', with its long, wooden handle, could be hurled half as far again. As for the Thompson sub machine gun, it may have served Al Capone well enough but it was a second rate infantry weapon.

In order to retain the initiative we patrolled aggressively non-stop, patrols to listen out in No Man's Land, patrols to ambush, patrols to draw fire which could then be pinpointed and replied to and patrols to cause mayhem and extract a prisoner or two for the purpose of identification. We mortared and machine-gunned our enemy and when he counter-attacked, for the first fortnight or so we could call up the navy and a cruiser or destroyer would blast away in support. Well out in front of our positions our highly trained snipers lay in wait along likely enemy patrolled paths. In the month they were actively engaged in this place our snipers registered at least twelve kills. For our part we had to put up with enemy mortar fire from multiple launchers loosed off a few hundred yards away. There was unending shelling by various calibres of gun and to begin with a good deal of bombing from the Luftwaffe raiding the beaches – their bombs tended to fall on us. Our method of reply to enemy mortars – which at one time seemed to be having things all their own way – was via a clever coordination of the mortars from all four commandos in the brigade whenever enemy fire was spotted at its source and this was managed quickly and accurately at one time in the proportion of ten of our bombs to every one fired by the enemy; later this fell to but never less than a three to one ratio.

We also had to deal with friendly fire. A naval rocket firing ship caught us still clearing an enemy position – which their faulty calculations told them we had left – and killed several unfortunate young men. A US squadron of medium bombers attacked us and for 20 dreadful minutes we thought we were done for. They dropped about 30 bombs, which missed us entirely, but their follow up machine-gun attack struck home and caused several casualties. Immensely impressive and exciting, though I believe without any particular success, was the British air assault on Caen which happened shortly after. Twice we saw and heard the entire strength of Bomber Command, 1100 aircraft each time, fly over us and a minute or two later drop some 20,000 tons of high explosive on that small town over two raids. To begin with anti-aircraft fire was enormous but it was soon overwhelmed. We could see bombers being shot down as they pressed their attack home. It was a sensational thing to watch but, as it turned out it was unsuccessful, for the Germans stayed put and their already strong defensive positions were improved by the massive debris left by the raids.

At the end of a week of hectic activity we were awarded a 12-hour break for sleep and a hot meal, which took place in small tents in a wet field in the pouring rain. In a nearby barn we discovered an ancient French gramophone with one needle and several dusty bottles of apple brandy. Before we embarked for France Fred and I had decided to take with us, concealed in our packs, two Bing Crosby records, 'Home on the Range' and 'Deep in the Heart of Texas'. 'Home on the Range' became a fatal casualty on landing but 'Deep in the Heart of Texas' survived until this exciting moment. Thirty of us gathered round and we were happily singing along with Bing and the apple brandy when several mortar bombs landed close by and that was the end of 'Deep in the Heart of Texas'. Everyone else survived more or less intact but sadly not the apple brandy.

The days went by in a non-stop whirl of minor upsets and foreboding. We fought both the Germans and the mosquitoes; we had some success against the former but the mosquitoes always won their battle with us. They made sleep difficult or well nigh impossible. They were a plague on us and when eventually repellents were issued they only attracted the wretched little demons even more.

Administratively we had continuing problems; we had each landed with a large pack, many of which had been lost or simply thrown away because their weight put one in danger of drowning. We had been sent out a minor change of clothing and also a great coat, which hardly came in handy on hot summer days spent in hedgerows and damp holes in the ground. Nothing really useful was received. Smart camouflage smocks as worn by the airborne troops replaced heavy coats eventually. We used them day and night.

Cooking was primitive as Commandos did not have officially trained cooks, and volunteers appeared from the ranks – two per troop of 60 men or more – who trained themselves as they went along. We mistrusted our particular cooks; they often had guilty expressions as if they were hiding something – our rations we suspected. We never felt satisfied after one of their meals and second helpings were unheard of. For a long time there was no fresh food and we lived on composite pack rations, 'Compo'. Whatever these were they were neither varied or much looked forward to. We were told not to ask the local inhabitants for food as they were probably starving. Who ever heard of a starving Norman peasant? They fed far better than we did, though they always showed great interest in our tinned Christmas pudding and could never get enough. We were glad to get rid of it. While the Americans cruised along happily with their daily ice cream and three star hotel food, we thought our best food was the thick wedges of corned beef sent up the line when it was too dangerous to cook, accompanied by mugs of surprisingly hot cocoa, laced on nights of unusual military activity with a good dollop of rum.

Marines traditionally had a daily rum ration. If you were under 18 or in the unlikely event of being teetotal you could opt for a small cash equivalent, which was paid when there was no regular rum ration during active service. When rum was doled out very occasionally in the cocoa there was a major attempt to deduct the daily money substitute paid on those days. It only just failed.

We were introduced at this time to defensive fighting which we had not experienced before. We were attached to the 6th Airborne Division, protecting the extremities of the beachhead. We laid mines and constructed wire entanglements, we dug deeper trenches with head cover from shells that burst in surrounding stout trees. Sandbags came in to use, along with camouflage, and we patrolled defensively, all quite new to us and the adjoining Commandos. One nearby unit was told it had a lot to learn in this respect and had in fact only reached page 34 in the infantry training manual.

Following the First World War there appeared in this manual an instruction on the distance infantry could be expected to charge a defended position without support or cover – it was 18 yards, in most instances still quite a long way. One very wet morning 3 Section were patrolling well in front of our line to investigate a reported enemy machine-gun position. We had a brand new second lieutenant with us who, when we spotted the gun and its crew of two, well dug in facing us and about a cricket pitch and a half away, gave the order to charge. Fred said, 'That gun is well beyond the 18 yards limit and we'll never make it,' but still our young firebrand insisted we charge, until one of the several Bills in the section and an old soldier via the siege of Tobruk and another one in Malta said quietly, 'We are not going, Sir, we are not disobeying your order, we are disagreeing from experience and superior knowledge, but either way we are not going. Nothing to stop you going though.' None of us went, we reported back to our mortars and they successfully took the problem over.

3 Section took part in many aggressive patrols, once in error supported by an entire brigade of artillery – some 48 guns. The section joined in looking devil-may-care for a documentary film shot by Gaumont British News reels. We once had a shower of what we had first thought to be eggs hurled at us over a hedge, which turned out to be an entirely new type of hand grenade. On one of our final patrols before changing position I came face to face with a steel-helmeted German emerging from a slit trench with his rifle pointing straight at me. In panic I shot him three times, but there was no reply or reaction and I advanced cautiously to find he had been dead several hours. A marine in another section was killed by a splinter from a mortar fragmentation bomb that had landed in a tree above his head; the splinter was so fine that there was no wound or mark whatever on his body.

Our daily routine was stand-to for an hour at 4.45am, then clean weapons, followed by breakfast. The hours before noon were spent improving positions wiring, gathering leafy head cover and a hundred and one other jobs. The afternoon was for sleep. In the evening any patrols that were going out that night were briefed, then in the hours of darkness double sentries were posted, patrols moved off and those without other employment took their ease along with the mosquitoes. Once in a while a few of us would cross Pegasus Bridge and bathe on the beach at Riva Belle or Luc, but there was no real peace anywhere or at any time, shellfire by day or night, and enemy aircraft unloading their bombs.

It is worth remembering that before D-Day the Commando had scarcely been in existence, only having had 80 days for formation, equipping and training. Soon we were all veterans or casualties. As we moved inland away from the beaches a few of us including 3 Section lost ourselves on our way back from a rather point-less patrol during which we had failed to spot an enemy mortar position and forgot the password to regain access to our lines. Regrouping and consulting our much used map, incorrectly as it happened, we became mixed up with a group of Canadians from Nova Scotia who told us a sad and chilling account of the shoot-ing of several Canadian prisoners of war in a nearby churchyard by members of the Hitler SS Youth Division. They were called out one by one by name into the churchyard and shot in the back of the head. They knew exactly what was going to happen to them and each man had shaken hands with his friends as his name was called out. Many years after the war the German officer concerned was still quietly living out his existence; he had been sentenced to death but this was finally commuted to life imprisonment from which he had been released in 1954 after serving only ten years. There were many SS who themselves were killed in that way in revenge or in some units as routine, which would account for the very small numbers who ever turned up in the prisoner of war cages. As far as the members of 3 Section were concerned we did our very best to behave reasonably, all of us having direct knowledge of this shooting of German SS prisoners, but our direct experience was limited to occasional intolerable battlefield situations in the wake of seeing our comrades die in sad and avoidable circumstances.

In early July, just after dawn and along with the mosquitoes, the enemy counter-attacked us in our newly strengthened positions. Counter-attacks were the very devil. It was fraught enough to have to take a well-defended position but to have to defend it almost at once from a vicious attempt to recapture it always came as wretched anticlimax. The German Army excelled in the art of counter-attack, often using fresh troops and they were always delivered depressingly soon after the initial fight. Nor would they be confined to a single attempt, far from it, so the original attack always involved several unpleasant fights not just to obtain but to retain a position as well.

On this occasion they came at us with four tanks, not Tigers but potent all the same. They shelled and machine-gunned us and there was the usual hail of flying splinters and ricochets going to and fro, but then they were caught out in the open and set on fire by our supporting 25-pounder battery firing at close range on rising ground less than a mile away. Their infantry had arrived from a flank in some force, spraying the area with an amazing rate of fire from their Spandau machine guns, but our medium machine guns were useful too and, with special ammunition, could range up to one and a half miles. We could only keep our heads well down shaking like jellies in our small narrow slit trenches, but we survived and indeed held our position thanks to our supporting guns. They were like a highly efficient fire brigade coming to the rescue.

Looking back on all this and thinking about similar events which were still to come, a major disappointment is that I never felt brave. I always felt scared out of my wits. Fear was ever present to a greater or lesser degree. Although I was highly trained and motivated, to such an extent it often seemed that nothing could possibly come close to the trials experienced while training, absolutely nothing prepared me for the regular appearance of an enemy extremely close and distinctly keen on killing me with bomb, bullet or bayonet. I volunteered for commando service because I was a schoolboy romantic and attracted to the heroic ideal of the fighter, at least I suppose that is what happened. Of course I may have been excited by the concept of the green beret and even by an article I read, categorically stating that commandos always had double rations.

I enjoyed my training but always found the active service part that followed, along with the fighting, very hard to absorb and cope with. My courage seemed to ebb and flow, never quite finite but certainly not infinite and it never, at least for me, remotely reached a heroic plane of endeavour. I used to regret that I never went forward for a commission but then I thought that was just as well – I would have been obliged to lead in front and at six feet four inches and in size 12 boots always stuck in the mud, I should have been a prime target for every hostile rifle and long since dead. So I got on with my job the best I could if far from brilliantly. I recharged my emotional batteries on a daily basis along with pals who may well have been in similar trouble and we all slogged on together. I think it was an American General who wrote about combat being easily definable into categories. He divided it into 'medal winning affairs' and the rest was relegated to minor episodes of military endeavour; utter rubbish of course. If you risk your life in war it matters little how many men are involved, you don't have to charge up a beach alongside thousands to be killed or maimed – it can be arranged in any multiple of one. The same General thought that every infantry section had a given proportion of the brave, the not so brave and downright cowards. The bane of my military life was the anxiety that I might be or might become a coward, though I probably confused cowardice with the extremes of fear that we all felt. In retrospect it was never cowardly to be frightened, it was how one managed it that mattered. The Roman army found that their youngest soldiers faired best in their first battle because they didn't know what to expect and stayed relatively fearless. Veterans on the other hand knew what was afoot and were always nervous. Eventually I became a veteran and remained apprehensive.

When I first experienced combat I approached it on an emotional tiptoe, but I stayed quietly confident until the first bullet whizzed past and the first dead body fell in front of me. Everything then changed and a new and frightening life got underway. Nor did I enjoy the assorted noises, the loud crack a rifle bullet made as it passed and the louder bang if it was close. Shells and mortar bombs whined, shrieked, howled, whistled and crashed about the place and quick-firing machine guns crackled and rasped away in demoralising fashion so rapidly were their bullets aimed or simply sprayed at you. High velocity rounds to knock you off your feet and fatally penetrate or wound. Tracers lit the sky so you could watch everything coming towards you. Explosive bullets, armour piercing ones and the further horror of an incendiary bullet which set its target on fire. And of course there were the endlessly flying random fragments of metal.

I came to always feel profoundly depressed before action got underway sometimes with an inclination toward bowel loosening or vomiting though neither actually happened to me. Afterwards I often felt totally deflated as if a giant vacuum cleaner had run over me. There was never any glamour in warfare.

In the middle of a fight I once felt an absurd desire to be playing cricket and more than once to be making love, mostly though, simple fear reigned and with it a feeling of acute, chronic tension. We used to call out to each other, 'Are you there Fred?'

'Where are you Nutty?' or I would hear Fred and other tough guys calling for their mums.

'Help, mum!'

I called for Jesus. We kept at it I think mainly because we cared for each other. I don't think England, home and beauty or even our regimental traditions had much to do with it, we simply had a very strong mutually felt need to look out for each other.

However, not all of us felt quite the same. We had among us several natural warriors who enjoyed fighting, were quite ruthless and seemed fearless into the bargain. I was lucky to have had Alastair McGonegal as my early mentor and bivouacking partner. He had been a Highland ghillie, moving effortlessly and silently with a bleak expression which veered between suspicion and out-right hostility. In Italy he had been put in charge of 40 prisoners who were placed under rather loose arrest in an amphitheatre sit-uation. They were at the bottom end of a distinct and quite deep hollow, with McGonegal on guard at the top. Although warned what would happen if they tried to escape, they attempted a break out on the first night and again on the second. On the third night they tried again and McGonegal – by this time very short of sleep – simply rolled four hand grenades down the steep slope and blew most of them up. I must say that though he often startled me almost as much as any enemy, I seemed to amuse him and he actually laughed once or twice. I had complete faith in his professional abilities, however savage he was, and thanks to him I learned how to make a waterproof bivouac in ten minutes and a mud pillow in five. It was McGonegal who gave me some special if unofficial advice.

'If you feel scared as you go to ground fire off five rounds rapid, at anything you like, the sun, the moon, the stars. Keep shooting, keep busy, keep your spirits up and when you have fin-ished firing always move to one side, some bastard is sure to have spotted your flash.'

Somewhere in between those who enjoyed fighting and those who found it far more frightening than they thought it would be, came the stoics, the majority. These were the survivors of countless fights, mostly cynics and 'know-alls', often droll men always ready to help and advise, sometimes at great length. They mostly seemed to come from the north, Wigan and Warrington, Huddersfield and Hull figured prominently. Bill from Bolton, who gave me his field dressing to bind up a wound, another Bill from Halifax who cut our hair and wanted to charge me double for having a rather full head, Nutty Slack our black marketer who always had a large supply of toffee and other sweets available for our pleasure (at a price) and George Moffatt who, when struck by flying shrapnel said, 'Goodness me! I believe I've been hit.'

These dauntless souls were our backbone. If the natural warriors and pirate captains gave the Commando its cutting edge, it was our stoics who held us together and made us laugh. If it was Napoleon who said that morale was more important than anything else in a soldier's armoury by three parts to one; these were the sorts of people he must have had in mind as prime providers.

They were not without a certain facility for complaining and grumbling in addition to being choc-full of all the required military virtues. At the end of an action, feeling fraught, short of breath, almost asleep on their feet and even too tired to eat, they would find energy for a loud and lengthy complaint if they felt unfairly treated or put upon. They disliked the early morning frontline routine of polishing cap badges which gave enemy snipers plenty of unlooked for opportunity, especially when the sun shone, and they were loathe to join in the physical exercise routines laid down as law by the new colonel. Excessive drill or any drill at all was regarded as an irrelevancy and a curse because of the nearness of the enemy. They felt that they were frontline soldiers and not on parade in barracks. The explanation that all this was vital for a tidy, disciplined, worthwhile existence made them very annoyed. Apart from all other considerations, they thought they had earned the right to relax from time to time, and not to be always clustered round a tin of polish and trying to keep a crease in their trousers.

One or two of our veteran stoics worked out how to use their letters home as a conduit to authority for their strongly held views on disciplinary matters. They knew that letters were censored by their troop officer, so they conducted their complaints in an indirect manner, along the lines that if the colonel only knew about all this he would have it put right at once. The letter's content would be conveyed to the colonel and eventually they would get their reply in the form of an official notice placed on a central notice board. It probably contained a confirmation of official policy but the complainants got a good deal of satisfaction from their ingenuity.

Cap badges apart, we also had trouble about what we should wear on our heads. Having spent our training gasping, literally, to get our hands on our green berets, we found ourselves spoilt for choice regarding headgear by the end of the campaign. We always wore berets whenever we could, although no enemy ever, as our instructors said they would, actually ran away at the sight of them. They were comfortable and we were proud of them but they often blew off. The alternative was a tin hat or steel helmet as they were meant to be called, left over from the First World War. These wobbled all over the head like pudding basins. There was a pleasing affair known as a cap comforter which looked smart, was made of wool and unravelled to reveal that it was also a scarf, but this blew off quite a lot. After about two minutes of being in action because of the flying fragments of metal we felt an acute need for something on top that would at least appear to keep shrapnel at bay. Of course nothing repelled an actual bullet but right at the end of hostilities a reasonably protective helmet was introduced and this gave us some extra confidence. It's failing was that in its prototype stage it was uncomfortable to wear and failed to give us the all-round protection over our ears and at the back of our necks that the German 'coal scuttle' helmets gave, and these had been going strong since 1914.

There was also the changing nature of the rest of our uniform. All infantry spend a large part of their time crawling along as close to the ground as they can, hoping they may remain hidden from their enemy for as long as possible. In this they gain some help from camouflage, their uniforms blending more or less successfully with the terrain. In times past when armies trudged to confront an enemy standing motionless some 50 yards away, soldiers wore uniforms in every colour of the rainbow to announce their presence and prop up all available courage ahead of mass slaughter at close quarters. However, along with the invention of the rifle came a pressing need to affect some sort of disguise and different armies chose varying shades and colours for their battle uniform. The British selected khaki, the Germans chose grey, and the French went in for various shades of blue, while later on a mottled series of patterns appeared on all kinds of material, protecting not only the soldiers and their weapons but also aeroplanes and battleships.

3 Section were rather sceptical about all this and made only minor exceptions to sartorial change. When we wore our absurdly out of date and inefficient steel helmets we were given lengths of string which could be fashioned to grip and cover the helmet and we would insert lengths of various forms of botanical substance to pretend that we were not really there at all. This did not work very well and we moved on to painting our helmets in a bravura system of colours not unlike some of Picasso's early work. We also carried camouflage scarves made from string, which we wound around our faces peering myopically through them before discarding them entirely. Eventually one good thing emerged from all this nonsense and that was the camouflage battle smock, which was issued only to Commandos and the Parachute Regiment. It replaced greatcoats and quite apart from its camouflage benefit became a highly prized fashion accessory and an absolute treasure at wet and windy post-war football matches.

A Lieutenant General came our way one very hot and steamy day, following heavy rainfall. Our local mosquitoes, despite a deluge of sprays, salves and ointments, were swarming everywhere. We were digging and hadn't seen him arrive. A smart young officer jumped out of the General's vehicle and dashed up to Fred shouting, 'Come on then, fall-in at once, the General wants to say a few words to you, hurry up and dress by the right.'

'We can see you do sir,' Fred incautiously replied and in we fell, mosquitoes buzzing menacingly round our ears. The General sneezed twice, blew his nose trombone fashion and launched into a nonsense speech full of tired phrases ending with, 'You are Royal Marines and that is honour enough for any man.'

Fred, in what he thought was a confidential whisper, said far too loudly 'to hell with honour, where's me bleeding' dinner?' The General heard this but surprisingly took no offence and as he drove off we heard him call out

'I hope your dinner arrives very soon, I'm sure you've deserved it.'

Although hardly relevant I thought of Kitty, our helpmate at home, and the story of her cheery scouse brother sitting beside his stretch of road at Ypres in 1915 with his fellow Liverpool Scottish drinking their methylated spirits and singing their awful songs at a passing horse-backed General:

Full of caprice and whim
He was tired of them
And they were tired of him

When we finished our digging we shuffled off to a small inn nearby and asked for cider. We were told it would have to be prepared and we would have to wait half an hour. We found it rough, enormously strong and very welcome. Fred drank deeply and lay down to doze in the nearby farmyard. He chose the pigsty for some reason and snored away with the best of them. The wife of the landlord saw him and sniffed rather haughtily in dismissal. The pigs all got up and disappeared, reminding me of folk singer Frank Crumit's famous song:

It was an evening in November
As I very well remember
I was gently strolling down the lane
My knees were all a flutter
So I lay down in the gutter
When a pig came by
And down beside me lay.
A lady passing by was heard to say
'You can tell a man who boozes,

By the company he chooses!'
And the pig got up and slowly walked away.

As so often in our lives, anti-climax arrived in the form of our Sergeant Major, a tall, thin, nasal Welshman, with the face of a bad tempered ferret and spirit to match.

'Get on with your digging', he ordered, 'Your dinner has been postponed indefinitely.'

A major problem facing officers and senior NCOs in the Royal Marines of that time was an inability to forget they weren't in peacetime regalia on board a battleship. Did they find their fighting men interesting, were they amused by them, did they enjoy their company as comrades? I don't think so. Far too much 'Royal' introspection. This failure or fear to relate was unfortunate, we were after all together in a difficult and unpleasant undertaking. Those who worked this out in a sensible, balanced way and acted in friendship were obeyed wholeheartedly, whereas others, who maintained a distant, even Prussian style of discipline, were disliked, often with negative results. The 1914–1918 dictum

Military discipline is a good thing
Too much praise a bad thing
- Make them try harder -

still held good in some commandos and ignored the ideal taught in training of self discipline. That is to say discipline from within, voluntarily and instinctively arrived at. A voluntary form of discipline breeds initiative, which was vital for the individual soldier whose job took him close to the enemy. Officers and NCOs who understood this reciprocal arrangement of self-help had no fear that their orders would not be followed, subject occasionally to a spot of informed discussion. They had no need to rant and rave at their men or act the bully.

My friend Fred, small, tough, loyal and intelligent, was continually undervalued and thought of as a disciplinary problem, while he was really an enthusiastic fine all-round soldier with marvellous resilience and sense of fun. 3 Section, connoisseurs of this sort of human being and hard to please, thought he was 'hot stuff' and they were right.

We were given another short break in the form of twelve hours of sleep and a bowl of hot stew, which was extended to a second night. I had heard a rumour that a Canadian battalion had moved into the line not far away – the Lorne Scots – my brother Michael's regiment and I set out to see if I could find him, Fred accompanying me. We set out in late afternoon carrying our rifles and six rounds of ammunition, five in the magazine and one 'up the spout', discouraged, but nearly always employed because it saved a couple of seconds on firing.

We followed what directions we had gleaned on our local grapevine and were finally directed to the relevant headquarters. I explained our mission but they were most unhelpful. 'But my brother really is in the Lorne Scots, he's a major,' I added helpfully.

'The hell he is get out of here,' was the reply. So we went. Down the road we found a pile of US Army rations in small sachets. They were labelled '2 bacon and one egg', 'bacon and two eggs', and 'ham and two eggs', all about three inches square, quite small and not unlike sachets of restaurant sauce.

We managed a brew-up and ate about 20 eggs with accompanying bacon between us. We felt no ill effects though the rations had no flavour and more than likely, in retrospect, the food should have been reconstituted. As it was now dark we bivouacked out in the open and went to sleep. We were awakened by bayonets prodding us and had a lot of trouble explaining who we were. I asked what regiment our tormentors were from but we were bundled off down the road again, told to go to hell and not come back. We supposed it was those Lorne Scots again.

My brother contracted tuberculosis soon after this escapade, about which he wasn't told, and was withdrawn from the active list. He had spent the cruel winter of 1940 with his fellow Canadians in a tent without warmth at Tattenham Corner on Epsom race-course. He succumbed to the illness a few years later.

We spent the rest of the night a few miles away down at the beach and in the morning I watched an old Tate and Lyle sugar barge phut-phutting ashore. It dropped its ramp as a small, smart looking sub-lieutenant in white tropical kit bounced out.

'I thought it would be much warmer,' he said. It was young Iain Robertson; we had shared a study at school.

'Have you ammunition aboard?' I asked.

'Good Lord, no. I have a much more important cargo than that, I've 2000 gallons of rum!' We shared some.

The next day was sunny following twelve hours of stormy weather and Fred, Grumphy Gough and I were standing in a squelchy, mud-filled ditch waiting for transport which we hoped would take us to a newly erected bathhouse. During the night a German patrol had come prowling and in the ensuing fire fight had left behind three dead bodies, which by midday had attracted so many flies we had to move them into another field. As we accomplished this, a despatch rider arrived to tell us the bathhouse excursion was cancelled and we were to expect a visit from a war reporter instead. An officer would be present to make sure we behaved ourselves.

Fred was upset about missing the chance of a bathhouse trip because he seemed to believe that where there was a military bath-house there would be a harem attached. He said they had them in the French and German armies but perhaps he'd got the wrong name. So we plodded along to the appointed crossroads for our meeting, caked in mud and thoroughly disgruntled. Grumpy car-ried the PIAT gun, I carted along its six heavy bombs and Fred was smoking two cigarettes. He always had a spare one tucked behind his ear ready to use but on this occasion he had lit both by mistake.

We arrived at the crossroads to find a smart green staff car await-ing us. There was no officer there but an energetic dapper little man shot out of the car and dashed towards us hand outstretched in genuine greeting.

'Hello!' he called out, 'I am a battlefield news reporter and I've come to interview you today because you are the closest of any soldiers in any of the Allied armies in Normandy to Berlin, the nearest Allied soldiers to Hitler himself. You are unique,' and he flourished a large map at us. 'There, you can see clearly, without question that you are geographically nearer to Berlin than any other soldier,' and in his excitement he reeled off several famous places in Berlin, to which we were apparently adjacent. 'Now then' he said producing pad and pencil, 'give me your names and addresses at home and I'll send your messages to your loved ones, carry on now,' he commanded and looked at Fred.

'Well,' said Fred, 'I haven't really got a sweetheart except for Daisy.'

'Excellent' replied our battlefield reporter. 'Let's have her full name and address, and don't forget your message.'

'Daisy's our cocker spaniel,' Fred replied, 'and you can tell her not to eat so many jellied eels, she's getting really fat.'

'I see, ha! Ha!' said the reporter joining in the fun and he turned to Grumpy.

'I haven't got a sweetheart either,' he said mournfully, 'unless you count Doris.'

'Well, what's her address?' he was asked.

'Oh, Doris, she's the wife, but you can give her a message, 'cos she goes out with Yanks see and you tell 'er that if she is still seeing them by the time I come home on leave I'll slit their throats from ear to ear and then I'll knock her bloomin' block off.' His interview dramatically completed, the battlefield reporter withdrew.

Sometime later I came across a copy of his paper and there in bold type was our interview, or most of it. It read something like this.

Today, I interviewed the fine cutting edge of the British Army, Commando soldiers and the closest of any Allied troops to Berlin, to Hitler's Chancery. Attacked during the night by superior numbers they fought off their enemy and with dead bodies piled all around them they will hold their positions indefinitely.

I showed it to Fred and asked him what he thought.

'Ah, well', he said 'there's no accounting for taste, I'd rather have had a go at that harem' and he gazed sternly into the distance with a somewhat gloomy expression.

'What's up Fred?'

'Oh,' he answered, 'I'm just trying to spot 'Inter der Bloomin' Linden.'

Fighting in Normandy involved dashing fearfully across narrow country roads and lanes, through thick hedgerows and on across unending small fields. Visibility was rarely more than 50 yards because of the giant hedges. Ambushes from almost impregnable defensive positions were easily set up by an astute enemy and were hard to spot in advance because of the canny use of camouflage.

Fred fired our Bren gun at a target towards the end of quite a large field, which he felt sure were Germans crawling along a hedgerow in early morning mist. His bullets struck home but when we reached the bodies we found to our dismay they were the bodies of our own soldiers killed in the recent attack and lying unburied.

3 Section were sent to check out a possible enemy machine-gun position, which proved to be entirely unoccupied. On our way back we struggled down a road that was mined and contained several booby-trapped gates into fields. We were almost caught in a mortar attack on an orchard we were about to pass through which shook us up badly. One moment everything was peaceful and seconds later apple trees were being blown up and fruit was flying all over the place. We came to a field that was hard to pass through safely because the hedgerows were so thick and it had no ditches to disappear into. We doubled back and were fired on from the far angle of the field. We let loose with our small section mortar, firing a 2lb bomb some 200 yards which, to our surprise, hit our target

first time and all hostile fire stopped. We fired off several smoke bombs and raced through the length of the field into a smaller one almost running into a German patrol coming the other way. We ran for a long deep ditch and agonised whether or not they had seen us. We noted that one of them carried a machine gun and another had an almost endless belt of ammunition wrapped around his body. There were only six of us and we had no automatic weapons. The enemy stayed where they were but detached two of their number to scout ahead.

We hoped they would all move on but the two scouts split up and began a detailed search of ditch and hedgerow. We crouched in the shade and hoped for the best. One of the scouts, a big burly chap with a sub machine gun, walked slowly along the hedge behind our ditch peering carefully as he went. We felt fairly sure he had seen us but could do nothing except crouch low and try not to imitate an unset jelly. Suddenly he ran to the end of the hedge, swung round and, opening fire, sprayed where he thought we were hiding, emptying a full magazine. Two of us were hit but as he paused to reload Fred stood up took careful aim and shot him in the chest. He fell with a crash almost on top of us. Our two casualties sadly proved fatal. One was Ginger, the undertaker's assistant and the other poor soul used to cut our hair at 3*d* per time. We took their name tags and the dead German's machine gun and fled through the back of the giant hedge and diagonally across the original field while the other scout tried to cut us down with burst after burst from his Schmeisser.

The rest of the patrol gave chase but the hedgerows were against them and soon they went back the way they had come, which is exactly what we did. As we reached the edge of the orchard we came upon a young lieutenant from one of the Yorkshire regiments cruelly injured by blast, which had ripped away his entire stomach. He stood against a tree, his entrails steaming on the grass in front of him. He was smiling as he tried to gather them together and stuff them back into his stomach before the shock killed him and he suddenly dropped dead. We were told it was his first action; it lasted perhaps ten minutes and followed two years of preparation and training.

I was summoned one morning to attend at headquarters a mile or so behind our front line positions where I found our Sergeant Major.

'I've been looking through your service record and see you are down as a student,' he told me. I remembered inserting that description because it sounded a lot better than runaway schoolboy. 'Well, I suppose you can work a typewriter then?' I said I had never tried but was told the regular clerk was away sick and I would just have to do my best.

I pounded away with one finger all morning, pausing with relief when a staff car pulled up outside, the office door swung open and in came the brigade commander, in short, a brigadier general. He asked for the troop commander and was put out to be told he had already gone to brigade to meet him, the Brigadier, 'by appointment' the Sergeant Major added critically.

'Never mind,' replied the General, 'this is only an informal visit and, by the way, I've just looked in on 3 Section – I think that was who they were' and he consulted a very formal looking notebook. 'Yes, that's right, Number 3 Section. I enjoyed my visit to them and came away quite invigorated.'

The Sergeant Major went a very pale shade of grey and held onto the table. 'I wouldn't have chosen them myself for a visit sir.'

'Why not?' asked the General. 'Well, sir, they're a poor lot, badly disciplined, always larking about, talking in the ranks, answering back a bad bunch.'

'Oh,' said the General thoughtfully, 'I noticed one of them wore the ribbon of the Military Medal.'

'That would be Marine Davies, he was awarded that before he got to us,' replied the Sergeant Major explaining away the award.

'And another,' continued the General remorselessly, 'had been mentioned in Dispatches.'

'Yes, sir, Marine Woods that was,' said our much unloved Sergeant Major in a tone of regret.

'Well' concluded the General, 'I have never before in my entire career come cross a body of men who after 48 hours of fighting in foul and filthy conditions all appeared early the following morning with immaculate creases in their trousers.'

'That would be Marine Woods, sir,' said the Sergeant Major, 'he does all their ironing.'

Harold Woods, who became Marine Woods, had been on duty on the steps of Portsmouth Guildhall in 1941 as a young police constable when the Luftwaffe almost demolished it and him. While others fled for shelter Harold stood fast giving first aid and encouragement and helping to evacuate the many casualties. His chief constable awarded him an important medal for gallantry and shook his hand. Harold, perhaps inspired by his busy time at the Guildhall, volunteered for commando service and that is more or less how he came to be with us.

He was ever so slightly camp, which in those days was not dwelt on very much. We felt he was a commando and one of us. He was always genial and he was brave. He also had a tenor voice of perfect pitch at a time when everyone in the unit fancied himself as Caruso or Crosby. He had a kitbag full of ancient dance band recordings plus a gramophone and was thus the leading member of our daily musical appreciation society. On top of all these accomplishments he was a dab hand with a needle and owned a genuine smoothing iron with which he managed our uniform repairs and creased our trousers – for a fee of course.

He only had one problem, in common with us all: the Sergeant Major disliked him, although that was really a point in his favour. To illustrate what an unpleasant man this strutting turkey of an NCO is shown by his behaviour to Harold who returned from a fighting patrol with a nasty wound to his wrist and arm.

'I've been wounded, Sergeant Major,' said the unfortunate Harold, his arm a mess of blood.

'Have you, Woods?' came the reply. 'How many arms have you got?'

'Two, Sergeant Major.'

'Well, carry on and use the other one.'

We were now very close to a German headquarters where, our intelligence operating accurately for once, advised that the entire stock of wines and spirits for supply to their army in the west was kept. Strenuous efforts to check this out were made by all Allied Forces who were in the area and many who were not. We did reasonably well, managing to liberate some Dutch gin, though this wasn't popular with everyone and in any case we were severely warned off further efforts. A full-scale assault on the town was turned down as a concept which some thought a pity. In the end the town concerned was bypassed and finally it surrendered to rear echelon troops, anonymous sort of chaps and probably all teetotallers anyway.

3 Section had a small problem before we moved off. We were patrolling along the perimeter in a small boat, necessary because the whole area was marsh, fen and tidal water. It rained a lot too. We pulled up for the night in what we felt sure was deep if inland water, unshipped our outboard motor and unwisely fell asleep. We woke up at dawn to find the tide had gone out and left us high and dry on top of a tall and extremely bristly hedge from which we had to make a muddy and perilous exit hauling the boat down after us.

Our turn came again to have another 'go' at what, for many infantrymen, was their least favourite military occupation – night fighting patrols. These involved a platoon, troop or company out and about in strange territory in the dark attempting deeds of daring for which they were not always equipped and couldn't see much point to anyway.

In the course of a moonlit night without camouflage or cover we sheltered in an old hay barn, partly to keep out of the rain and partly to set up an ambush for the enemy who were known to use it as an observation point during the day. Dawn was breaking, it continued to rain heavily and we found the Germans were already there in some strength.

It came as a surprise to both sides and in the violent fire fight that followed the barn was set ablaze and everyone involved shot at each other in panicky abandon. Fred and I evacuated the building and leapt into a nearby ditch, which was already inhabited by three Germans who thankfully fled. Fred flung a phosphorus grenade after them which set fire to that part of the barn still standing. Any remaining enemy having vanished, we managed to collect ourselves together and set out on our main objective of the evening to relieve some Polish infantry positioned well ahead on a mythical compass bearing that no one understood.

We did find them but only because they opened fire on us unexpectedly and introductions were extremely fraught and difficult. They finally evacuated their main trench and, in the half-light of dawn, 3 Section dropped gratefully into it. There was a gruesome sticky feeling as our ankles disappeared into what we thought might be the effects of prolonged wet weather. But further research and an awful stench revealed to be at least a week's worth of faecal matter. The concluding diagnosis was that the Poles had used one half of their trench as a latrine and the other half for cooking. Three cheers for night fighting patrols.

While I am thinking of Poles in wartime it seems apt to mention one of our number called Terry Schofield who, by an intricate system of recruitment, had come to us via the Merchant Navy, where he had manned a gun on the stern of an armed merchant ship and was torpedoed while lighting his pipe of 'Three Nuns'. He survived his time as a commando and after the war became a prominent executive member of SSAFA, a charity for distressed soldiers, sailors and airmen. Terry was told by his directors to place special emphasis on helping Allied servicemen. He found two ancient Poles who were desperately hard up and told him how they had fought, indeed been wounded and taken prisoner in Normandy. He told head office and they were delighted.

They told him to send pictures, which Terry did. He even borrowed a Polish flag from the British Legion as a backdrop. As a result they were invited down to London to Horse Guards to watch Trooping the Colour. Terry filled them up with Polish beer and Schnapps and after the performance they met Prince Philip, were taken to a West End show and had their pictures taken by several magazines and newspapers.

At their hotel the following morning the SSAFA chairman said, 'A word with you Schofield, about those two Poles of yours.'

'Yes, sir' said Terry, 'anything wrong?'

'Well, as a matter of fact there is, they did fight as they said, they were wounded and taken prisoner, but it's just that they fought for the Germans.'

But back to that trench. With regard to the British Army's attitude to sanitation – in contrast to that of the Poles – its field regulations instructed that sanitation was to be observed with almost as great a degree of priority as dealing with the King's enemies. I remember the esoteric diagrams that circulated showing latrine details according to length of stay, type of ground prevailing etc and I certainly recall with dismay the casual efforts of some of our allies with respect to both sanitation and hygiene.

I remember being surprised at the many uses found for old biscuit tins and, in a small book on military sanitation dated 1912, I noticed that a battalion of 700 men were responsible for 250 gallons of urine daily, equivalent to 1500 bottles of wine. Another slightly bizarre fact which registered was that in 1917, 180,000 men assembled to fight a battle which lasted a month and yet only a week after they left the area, so efficient was the cleaning up sanitation effort that it was difficult to see that a colossal battle had taken place at all. I think our rule was never to behave like the Poles we came across but simply to hope for the best when in an area under shellfire or when snipers were about.

One very early morning patrol in front of our position – accompanied by several hundred mosquitoes – revealed the surprising fact that there was no sign at all of any enemy troops of any kind in any direction; they had disappeared entirely overnight. We reported back at once to our 'l'eminence gris', at troop head-

Pupils at Repton School playing football *c.*1938/42.

Some of the tools of the trade: a knuckleduster of 1942; a Middle East pattern knuckle-knife; the famous Fiarbairn-Sykes Fighting Knife and the Smatchet knife used by Commandos.

The author abseiling down a 100-foot cliff during commando training in the Scottish Highlands.

Eisenhower's letter to the troops before D-Day.

Commando briefing en route to Normandy for D-Day.

D-Day landing craft. Its crew of three worked and slept on board for weeks on end. In a similar craft 32 Marines drowned in a storm returning from Normandy.

Above: A small infantry landing craft at sea on its way to Normandy. (IWM B5098)

Left: A landing craft depositing infantry on a Normandy beach. (IWM B5092)

48 Commando's headquarters landing on D-Day. Note the ridiculously spindly ramps off which a Marine carrying heavy equipment is falling. (IWM B5219)

Commandos landing from a small assault craft on D-Day. (IWM B5245)

A D-Day beach scene early in the day. (IWM B5114)

Commando reinforcements coming ashore on D-Day with blackened faces.
(IWM MH33547)

A Sherman tank concealed in a hedgerow in Normandy.

48 Commando Bren gun team in action on D-Day. The gun sight is set for close quarter fire. (IWM B5057)

Taking prisoners on D-Day.

Prisoners being guarded The situation doesn't look too good for them but they seem relaxed.

Commandos assembled away from the beach late on D-Day. (IWM B5058)

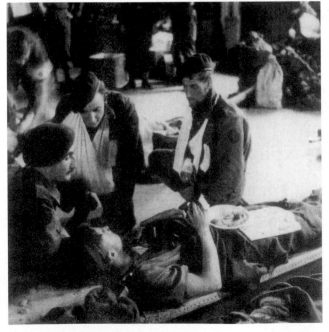

Commando forward dressing station, Normandy, perhaps half a mile from the fighting.

Hitler Youth SS prisoners in Normandy. They were quite amazingly fanatical and few were taken prisoner.

The welcoming committee for the liberating Commandos in Normandy. This was exceptional, as in the days after D-Day we found that the locals disliked us and many opposed us quite strongly.

Smoke over Walcheren as battle rages, November 1944.

A landing craft sinking with its crew abandoning ship after being hit by shore batteries. She went within 50 yards of a German pill box and received point blank hits. Walcheren, November 1944.

A captured German Spandau machine-gun in use against them. (IWM CC1397)

The two light machine-guns: on the far sides is the Bren gun, which fired 600 rounds per minute. On the near side is the German Spandau which fired 1200 rounds per minute; it only took five seconds to change its barrel in action.

The Schmeiser sub machine-gun. 'Simple, deadly, still in use.'

'The Patrol Returns', in this case after several days on Dutch Island rescuing a senior (and very unpopular) officer, lost behind enemy lines. Kneeling is Lance-Corporal Tickle, our gallant medal-winning pacifist medical orderly.

4 Commando being addressed by Lord Lovat. Note that they are wearing cap comforters.

48 Royal Marine Commando at Minden in June 1945.

U.B. NO. Wolverhampton 163 317
R. 23 (Revised—June, 1942)   'Volunteer'   Entered for the period of the present emergency   Sta. 10169/42   R.M. 163/6/42. A.I.
FULL NAME McALPINE Kenneth Scott (Surname in Block Letters)   DIVISION AND REGISTER No. Po/X 1148/L

Date and Place of Enlistment — 9 September 1942 At Exeter Barracks
Date and Place of Birth — 30 March 1925 At Liverpool in Lancs.
Trade Brought Up To — Student
Date of Re-Engagement
Religion — Church of England
Date of Marriage

NEXT OF KIN
Relationship
Name
Address

Description of Person — Feet 6 Inches 1½ Chest Ins. death Hair Brown Eyes Blue Complexion Fresh — Marks, Wounds and Scars: Molar scar near 1st index finger

FORMER SERVICE ALLOWED — To reckon towards GCB, Pay and Pension: In what Service, Yrs. Days
Good Conduct Badges — Date 30-3-46 1st Granted Grantee 2nd Deprived 3rd Restored

Employment During Service — From, To, From, To, Nature
Medals, Clasps and L.S. and G.C. Gratuity — Date: ISSUED 10/8/1950 — Nature of Decoration: 1939–45 STAR, FRANCE AND GERMANY STAR, DEFENCE MEDAL, WAR MEDAL

Wounded on War Service — 29-8-45 — R.W.C. and War Gratuity Authorised

The author's service certificate.

Memorial to the dead of 48 Royal Marine Commando.

The Commando war memorial in the Scottish Highlands close to Ben Nevis where we trained in somewhat bleak and austere conditions.

The author's battle smock, currently on display at the Royal Marines Museum, Portsmouth.

The author wearing his battle smock and green beret.

quarters and were told to go out again and take an officer with us which the section immediately did with the same result. Later that August day of 1944 and accompanied by our intelligence officer, it became obvious that the Germans were involved in a major movement to their rear areas heading west towards Le Pont l'Eveque. The entire brigade hurtled after them and 3 Section for better or worse led the way and in no time at all became involved in heavy fighting with the enemy rearguard defending a fortified farmhouse alongside an important set of crossroads close to the small town of Dozule.

As we approached the farm buildings along a narrow dung-filled lane a German staff car shot out of the main building at great speed towards us. Our light machine gun neatly positioned ahead of the section in a nearby ditch opened up on the car with a full magazine and it careered past us before suddenly slewing to a halt heavily tilted to one side. I was first on the scene partly because I had dropped behind to repair an errant bootlace; I therefore approached the car at the same moment as an enormous SS officer emerged from a rear seat. He must have been a yard or so away from me and I shot him twice as he raised his pistol to do the same to me. A bullet then whacked into the roof of the car just above my head and a familiar voice close by said, 'Sorry Lofty, I missed him.' The voice belonged to Alf Allday from Cornwall who oddly enough had won prizes for his marksmanship but had a dreadful stammer which was inclined, as he talked non-stop, to put him off when snap shooting. Having disposed of the staff car and removed an expensive looking watch from the wrist of the much decorated German officer lying dead across the car bonnet we turned our attention to the sky above the farmhouse where two Spitfires were rather ominously circling, when a Spandau fired a long and menacing burst at us from the farmhouse roof.

Just then several Nebelwerfer rockets fell almost amongst us with their weird howling and moaning crash bang and wallop noise, but luckily they hurt no one except two cows waiting to be milked. The Spitfires now came quite low overhead, so assessing the risks between being killed by the irate machine-gunner or torn to pieces by the Spitfires' rockets, bombs and cannon we opted in favour of the latter and rushed out onto some grass at the side of the farmhouse, waved our green berets madly above our heads and shouted rather pointlessly at the top of our voices 'Clear, off – we are friends.' The leading Spitfire responded at once, loosing off four large and deadly cannon shells which zipped past us, missed the farmhouse but struck its adjoining giant haystack which erupted into flames with a great deal of unpleasant smoke. The second Spitfire pushed off home, but the German machine gun continued firing at us while another one opened up, pinpointing our position from the far side of the building. Feeling hot, dusty and desperate we trundled our clumsy PIAT gun into position in a ditch 30 yards from the front door of the building and successfully loaded its complex apparatus, fired it three times – itself a major physical triumph – and blew the farmhouse to bits.

A white flag on the end of a stick appeared from amongst the ruins followed gingerly by eight members of the Hitler Youth 12th SS Panzer Division. They said they had left the same number in the ruins. We debated what to do with them – we had no transport and armed or unarmed they posed a threat – we couldn't simply let them wander away. The only wartime battle solution seemed to be to shoot them and rightly or wrongly that was nearly their fate when our Padre arrived driving his specially converted church service truck. Complete with an escort we handed over our prisoners to the Lord's representative and trudged away from the ever so slightly damaged farmhouse. We probably hoped to see the Commando charging across the fields waving celebratory flags and shouting 'hosanna' or at the very least 'hurrah', but all we found was brigade headquarters which appeared to be busy moving into a fine looking chateau. They said we looked a mess and when we requested food they gave us each a bag of raisins and a small tin of Christmas pudding. For the second time we came across our intelligence officer now waiting to interview the prisoners we had just captured. He showed no interest at all in us or we in him.

Our rendezvous with our troop headquarters had been fixed for midnight via a complicated series of map references we would have to follow in the dark. We felt fairly confident about this because Harold our section Lance Corporal had once escaped during or shortly after the Siege of Tobruk in 1941 in North Africa and claimed to have made his heroic way across the desert and back to safety, navigating by 'the stars, the sun and the moon'. He made it sound as if they all came out together and stayed put for his personal guidance.

We spent all night rambling through the totally dark countryside, neither Harold his compass or any form of stellar navigation helping at all before we finally threw ourselves down in complete exhaustion and fell asleep. When we woke at dawn and prepared to move off we smelled burning timber and lo and behold found ourselves back at the old farmstead; we weren't enormously pleased with Harold.

Our travails of that day and night almost had a happy ending; we bumped into divisional headquarters who were also lost but who were about to take over – for their greater comfort – an entire Norman castle. One of their minions awarded us very comfortable billets overnight but as we moved in prior to sleeping on actual beds for the first time in three months, they rudely turned us out onto the nearby village street and took over our billet for themselves. Call it divine justice if you like but we heard later that on moving in and before tucking themselves up for the night, two of their number opened some drawers without checking, discovered they were booby trapped and spent the next few weeks in hospital.

Our next obstacle was to be the River Seine at its Duclair Bend inland from Le Havre and north of Vernon. We moved up to the river at the end of August and witnessed a terrible sight where German SS troops not far ahead of us, trying to cross the river by ferry had been caught and largely obliterated by RAF Typhoon fighter bombers. It was a profound relief not to have to fight them on the other side of the river but a grim fate for all that. On a lighter note we came across an undamaged 56-ton German Tiger tank intact, except for having run out of fuel. Fred climbed on board, lifted the turret lid and disappeared inside reappearing a few minutes later with an enormous black and red swastika flag, which he draped around himself and waved about dancing on top of the tank. Someone using a captured camera took several snapshots of the scene which no doubt enlivened its owner's family album in the years ahead.

We crossed to the right bank of the river with its strong current in small assault boats. One group travelled in a Welsh coracle which went round and round in diminishing circles more or less across the entire span of the river; luckily there were no defenders on the far side. Heading for Le Havre we endured some impressively awesome big gun shelling which threw up vast clouds of dirt though caused little damage. We were mortared and a shower of rockets whistled down too close for comfort, while a steady rain poured down on everything.

We rescued a large consignment of Camembert cheese from an overturned lorry, which made a welcome change from unending tins of corned beef and Christmas pudding. No one in 3 Section had ever tasted Camembert and we didn't much care for it, especially Fred who said it tasted like cow dung; someone called Arthur asked him how he knew. Late in the day and soaking wet the foraging section came across a large party of the enemy complete with their machine gun at a bend in the small track we were following. We crawled through a large hedge, came up on their flank unseen and killed five of an assortment of German and Polish troops, capturing one of the Poles who said he and his compatriots wanted to surrender but feared the Germans would shoot them. About this time after several rockets had arrived in the area with a tremendous 'whoooosh' someone waved a white flag from a hedge and a head appeared, but this was followed by the bang of a rifle and both the head and the white flag disappeared. A nearby unit reported that a Polish soldier was so relieved to have been taken prisoner he embraced their Sergeant Major and kissed him on both cheeks. It certainly wasn't ours.

At a village called St Leger Duboscq we attacked another German machine-gun position behind a thick strong hedge, firing smoke bombs from the small section mortar and reappearing more or less behind them almost exactly as described in the official infantry training manual page 27. Our haul here was six enemy killed with the same number captured and in addition four abandoned guns, six four-wheeled artillery wagons and thirteen horses of various sizes. We could never see more than a field away – tall hedges were a wretched hindrance, providing cover for camouflaged enemy machine guns often firing on pre-set lines down and sometimes through them unexpectedly. One assault on a position protected by a thick hedge and barbed wire ended in disaster when a comrade from a nearby section became impaled on the defending wire while an unlucky rifle shot hit the phosphorus grenade held on his belt. It proved impossible for his friends to free him from the grenade and its fiery and explosive slow burning contents literally burnt into his body. It was a desperately awful situation, which was ended by his best mate shooting him in response to his agonised cries and requests to end his misery.

We now began to leave behind a battlefield of hedgerow and ditch, of huge earthen barriers fortified by complex weaving together of tree roots, brush and branch. Colossal impenetrable hedges that lined every field giving major advantage to a defending force who sat secure in their positions lobbing mortar bombs at us and blazing away with machine guns down the very narrow roads and tracks along which we mainly advanced. On a lighter note both Fred and Arthur developed bad blisters on their feet and decided to try out the enemy style of footwear, namely jackboots removed from various casualties. This went well, especially when they found clean socks and a bar of soap in an abandoned house. Rubbing the soap vigorously onto the socks they soon marched free from both corns and blisters, only to fall foul of the Sergeant Major who disliked the jackboots.

We had now marched for six days across rough country, facing the enemy each day and most nights without any proper sleep for

96 hours; many of us fell asleep on our feet when forward motion ceased. We were ready for a rest and were finally given one at a small place just short of Le Havre called St Maclou, where to our astonishment the Plymouth divisional band of the Royal Marines turned up and in pouring rain caused a major sensation amongst the local population and indeed ourselves. The band was on its way to play in liberated Paris. On another day George Formby and his wife made a welcome visit as we neared Dunkirk. This indefatigable entertainer had also visited us right up in our front line positions not long after D-Day. The applause after the show on that occasion was so great we all hastened underground in case of enemy retaliation.

About mid-September we all arrived at Le Havre where our job seemed to be to act as a police force following its recent capture, with the major attraction being protecting the stores of food, wine and ammunition from looters. The main difficulty was that here assembled in one huge store were all the wines and spirits belonging to the entire German Army in Western Europe. We weren't there very long which was a relief; we were having more fights within the ranks than with our official enemy, and then there was Danny Ryan our most recent member of 3 Section. Danny's family – though living across the road from our home barracks in Portsmouth – originated from County Cork and had been apple growers. His mother had persuaded Danny to promise he would forsake all alcohol until he was 21 – at this point he still had two years to go. He often consulted a treasured photo of his staunch teetotal mother in which she appeared to be having a bit of a knees-up, sporting what looked like a large glass of red wine and having a very happy time indeed. Danny assured us it was only tonic wine in the photograph and seemed not to think of it as wine in the sense of it being alcohol. We happened to be in Benedictine liqueur country, its source of manufacture being just up the road at Fecamp, and Fred got hold of a flagon of the stuff which we all imbibed in very large glasses except for Danny. However, someone filled Danny's glass to the brim with Benedictine and told him it was

Dandelion and Burdock. Being a nice simple soul Danny drained his glass, rose from the table, pirouetted three or four times in a neat little circle and fell flat on his face. He recovered some twelve hours later but unfortunately had acquired a taste for alcohol – particularly Benedictine. When the war was well and truly over we all met Danny's mother when she came to the Barracks to welcome him home. She gave us a lovely party in a room with bright yellow wallpaper above a pub next to a fish and chip shop. She gave us all a big kiss and thanked us for looking after Danny and we all, including Danny, drank lots and lots of lovely tonic wine.

We removed ourselves from Le Havre and headed towards Dunkirk. Hitherto our reception had varied, withdrawn and often hostile early on in Normandy where the population had lived with the German occupying force for years, then as we advanced westward people were cordial but not effusive for there was still a feeling of resentment at the fighting and damage to their homes, but now all was different. Each unscarred town or village turned out to welcome us waving and throwing flowers, Pavilly, Yerville, Motteville, Valmont and others produced marvellous scenes of rejoicing. Fred was hit in the face by a bunch of roses thrown at the jeep in which he was travelling at 40 miles an hour and managed to laugh while everyone crowded around when we stopped, pressing wine, cider, fruit and bread on us.

We met no enemy opposition; the local Resistance dashed about occasionally bringing us stray prisoners including a fair haired SS man who had pictures of Hitler with himself standing as a bodyguard in the background. When one rather weedy looking youth was brought through the streets of one town, loud jeers arose from the crowd and he was barely saved. We were still on foot most of the time, marching doggedly along with renewed blisters and corns. At Valmont we had our best reception of all, being awarded civilian billets. Arthur said 'Quite like home'. Fred told him he couldn't have had much of a home then. They never really got on.

Dunkirk was strongly garrisoned and almost entirely surrounded by water. It had been decided to contain the town rather than assault it and our Commando brigade some 2,500 strong took over a front of 10,000 yards from an entire Canadian division. To deceive the enemy into thinking that the Canadian armoured car regiment we had relieved was still there, for some unknown reason we were told to turn our berets inside out with the black lining uppermost. Our defensive positions, as we lacked the mobility of armoured cars, were each separated from the other by several miles and surrounded by floodwater, and from then on we resumed serious warfare. We received spasmodic support from the Resistance some of whom were communists who came down from as far as Lille. We were told they were useful even if in practice they were unpleasant and completely useless. I think what impressed us most at both Le Havre and Dunkirk was that we started to receive fairly regular and even at times, hot meals again, our supply services having finally arrived within striking distance.

Vickers machine guns came in handy firing their new long-range ammunition. Our enemy knew they could reach up to one and a half miles but thought more than that was beyond them so they were always being caught out and suffered quite severe casualties. We now had several fierce patrol actions which reminded those of us who had forgotten that lesser battles can get you killed as easily as the major ones. We didn't have to contend with much shellfire except for the wretched air bursts neatly timed and spaced directly over our heads, but we were mortared, machine-gunned and sometimes outwitted.

An example of the latter occurred one misty September morning when we were sent to bombard an enemy-held farm with our PIAT gun. We spotted three Germans working in a field only 40 yards away; we didn't open fire quickly enough and several enemy Spandau light machine guns opened on us from alarmingly close by. We then fired at the three Germans who were seen to drop, our Vickers guns firing at extreme range but missing all their targets, and when we fired our PIAT at the farm it jammed and a Spandau we weren't aware of suddenly fired at us from barely two cricket pitches away and with its first burst hit two of the PIAT party –

which for the first time in several outings didn't include me. We then hastily withdrew under covering fire from our two Bren light machine guns, their party incurring two wounded.

The enemy now began to shell and mortar the area, forcing us to withdraw in confusion to a nearby field of unharvested potatoes. Here a field gun began firing uncomfortably close by, distributing its unwelcome air bursts over our heads. We finally arrived back at our starting point after five hours, carrying our casualties with some difficulty over wet and muddy terrain. We had two comrades killed and three wounded. The following night we went out again, the PIAT delivered three bombs on target and destroyed the farm without casualties. A further patrol ran into severe trouble when ambushed in thick mist in another fortified farmhouse and suffered casualties. Our enemy didn't lose all the smaller battles.

Sadly we lost Dennis in one of these skirmishes, killed by a roof top sniper. He was older than the rest of 3 Section and had actually got his civilian career underway before joining up as a volunteer; like myself he had refused a chance of a commission. He had had an interesting job as a wine salesman dealing in ships' stores, delivered under bond to Royal Navy warships mostly at Christmas. Dennis had a nice story of calling one Christmas Eve on an ocean-going submarine at Rosyth on the Firth of Forth. He completed his business, was well entertained afterwards by both Captain and crew and woke up much later in Gibraltar. When we commiserated with him he said 'Oh there was nothing to worry about I just caught the next submarine home again.' Many years later as a wine merchant I called on an RAF bomber base in Lincolnshire; it was the main headquarters for the 'V' or Valiant bombers carrying the country's nuclear deterrent at the time. I was offered a trip in a Valiant and happily accepted. We became airborne and sitting next to the pilot I heard loud crackling from the radio followed by what sounded like a coded message. My pilot replied to the message 'Tally Ho then – we're on our way.' When I asked where we were going, he replied 'Sit back; we're off to bomb Moscow'.

7

September 1944: Walcheren

We were glad to leave Dunkirk, excessive floods and marshland had only limited appeal and beating up fortified farmhouses with the ridiculous PIAT and shooting the German occupants even less. We had started to take large groups of prisoners who we felt were really trying to desert. Militarily from the point of view of 3 Section it was a complete dead end and we much looked forward to having dry feet again. So we were withdrawn at the end of September 1944 to train for an assault on the island of Walcheren, which we were told blocked the entrance of the river Scheldt to our shipping. This was to involve fighting over sand dunes, and a suitable training area was found at de Haan in Belgium where there had once been heavy German coast defences embedded in its similar sand dunes. There was also to be comfortable accommodation in abandoned private houses in the area. This had great appeal though the assault itself when it came proved a trifle disillusioning.

THE PURSUIT

1. On June 6th we came to Normandy. We seized the bridges, the Le Plein Le Mesnil high ground and Ranville areas.
2. What we seized we held.

3. For two months we sat on the defensive while the General Montgomery's great plan unfolded itself.

4. On August 17th we started a grim pursuit. Since then we have advanced 40 miles. This is an average of 7,000 yards a day as the crow flies; as the troops have had to march it has been half as far again.

5. We have fought and beaten the enemy at Cabourg, Goustranville, Dozule, Branville, Annebault, Pont l'Eveque, Equainville and Beuzeville.

6. In this fighting we have lost many good friends. We have, all of us, at times been tired and weary.

7. We have fought side by side with our gallant allies the Belgians and the Dutch. THE GREEN AND THE RED BERETS HAVE FOUGHT AS ONE. 150 and 191 Field Regiments and 60 Heavy Anti-Aircraft Regiment has supported us splendidly, effectively and loyally.

8. I congratulate you on your great achievements: On your stamina, on your skill and on your grim determination.

9. The motto of the 6th British Airborne Division is 'Go to it'. You have gone to it and right splendidly you have done it.

RICHARD A GALE

Major General

Commanding 6th British Airborne Division

26th Aug 44

I remember very little about de Haan except thinking it would make a pleasant little seaside resort to visit in peacetime, but then I had much the same feelings about the Normandy watering places we had invaded on 6 June. I do recall a quite dreadful smell the Section stumbled on which we thought must be the scene of some appalling atrocity, which, contained inside two enormous steel boilers turned out to be a vast quantity of unused soup. We started training over the dunes in light unarmoured amphibious vehicles called Weasels, which were meant to be able to go over anti-tank mines without detonating them. They went well on land but were hopeless in water and far from foolproof as far as the mines were concerned. We were also introduced to tracked landing vehicles known as Buffaloes in which – whether it was their fault or not – we barely survived and in using them were killed in fairly large numbers. We trained vigorously amongst the dunes, especially reviving the use of our bayonets which we hadn't much thought of in recent battles, and discussed at length whether to wear steel helmets, woollen cap comforters or green berets. The cap comforters were chosen and we quite approved as they unrolled into nice warm scarves; in the event they all blew off, as did our berets. Our bayonets did come in handy but at that time were only short metal spikes and not much thought of. Tommy guns, grenades and rifle shots from the hip were the preferred weapons of assault. Someone found a map showing large numbers of minefields likely to be found on Walcheren and we noticed on the accompanying fire plan many numbered circles denoting mortar targets, an effective system of prearranged fire zones.

An important admiral came along to address senior officers and news filtered down to the grass roots that he had told Montgomery he ought to have cleared the approaches to Antwerp before considering Arnhem, but had been turned down which had made opening up the port of Antwerp very urgent apart from its effect on the Arnhem landing itself. I don't think any member of our small section felt especially motivated or full of good cheer over what lay ahead – in fact I am quite sure none of us thought of it as other than just one more bloody battle but this time vastly more dangerous than anything since the Normandy landings. Still, we attended the Chaplain's service the afternoon before we sailed from Ostend and had a good go at our pre-battle hymn reserved for these occasions. We tried hard not to wonder what the morning might bring.

The amphibious assault on Walcheren Island was undertaken on 1 November 1944 in order to free the approaches to Antwerp and to allow massive supplies – previously coming from as far away as Cherbourg – a simpler entrance towards the fighting in Holland and subsequently Germany. It was the second major battle for 48

Commando following its D-Day tribulations and it was a major battle because all three services were heavily involved. The Royal Navy sent along a battleship and two odd vessels dating back at least to the First World War called monitors, each carrying two heavy bombardment guns. The RAF eventually provided heavy bomber support and importantly, mobile artillery in the form of fighter bombers, while a marvellously brave separate group of assorted landing craft – nearly all destroyed in the preliminary fighting – were there to cover the landings. The British Army and Canadians fought to invade the island from its Dutch side but the actual assault was carried out by three Marine and one Army Commando, in all some 2500 strong and in precise terms of the assault and the next several days of combat on the island itself they faced and defeated a total enemy force of about 10,000. It was indeed a major battle.

At full strength a commando of that time was approximately 450 men composed of five fighting troops (now called rifle companies) of 70 men each, a support troop of 40 manning two medium machine guns and two mortars and a headquarters troop composed of all sorts of specialists including signallers and engineers. However by the time Walcheren came along our Commando was well below total strength; there were really not enough of us. The problems involved were known to be considerable – the island was very heavily defended against assault by sea and its tactical importance was obvious so beyond local surprise none could be expected. In addition it was now November and rough seas were more than likely.

The plan was that the main sea dykes must be breached and the interior of the island flooded. At the same time the shore batteries would have to be neutralised by a pre D-Day bombardment and all field batteries put out of action by air attack and the assaulting naval bombardment. The main opposition to the Commando was a coast defence battery of four heavy concrete-entrenched guns along with a sizable infantry force and ample support from deadly mortars. The terrain surrounding the landing area was made up of high dunes of inconveniently loose sand providing endless problems over the efficient use of both rifles and light machine guns, which were subject to constant jamming. There was no armoured vehicle support though we came across several derelict tanks that had got stuck coming ashore. The 25 craft of the support force varying in size from 10 to 100 tons were almost all disabled or destroyed. They had managed to knock out two of the 26 large German guns opposed to them but had been matched against far stronger defences than they were designed to overcome.

H-Hour for the assault was fixed for 10am on Sunday 1 November; the sky was grey and stormy looking and the sea was surprisingly calm. Bomber Command had breached the dykes and flooded the island but no final supporting raids took place because of extensive fog over English airfields. Apart from our own weapons we received no effective fire support for several hours, unless the attempted help from a naval rocket-firing craft can be counted when an electrically fired salvo of 100 rockets came down not on the beach defences but very nearly alongside us. The water around us was full of bursting explosives; we passed one craft which had been hit – it was stopped and listing heavily and badly scorched by blast, the blame for which was later put down to faulty primitive radar. The errant rocket craft was itself hit shortly after, exploding in a sheet of flame.

There was now heavy shellfire as we approached the beach and a hail of splinters arrived aboard our amphibious vehicles before we could make it into the shelter of the dunes. We looked around us to assess our position. The shelling had increased and the 800 shells per gun of the coastal batteries were being hurled at the approaches to the island and the landing area with frightening intensity. A major craft carrying our mortars and machine guns took a direct hit, a shell exploding against the armoured front of one of the vehicles aboard. The driver and wireless operator were killed and two machine-gunners were badly wounded. Their guns were still on board when the landing craft was compelled to put off from the beach to avoid further shelling. An officer and two marines managed to swim ashore with two tripods but no guns. The craft then struck a mine trying to go alongside a hospital ship and sank. Another large craft got stuck blocking the best exit from the beach inland and proved immoveable while many amphibians were set ablaze as they tried to work their way round the landing area towards a safer approach.

At that moment there came scrambling breathlessly up the dunes some 70 marines breaking clear from the worst of the shelling and bringing with them their more than welcome machine guns and a surprisingly large supply of barley sugar which was to be our main source of food for the next two days. The terrible shelling continued to be fierce and accurate and we watched an amphibious vehicle lurch to a halt and sink in the sand; its ammunition caught fire and a marine stood up perilously to hurl the burning boxes into the sea.

As we moved forward crawling across the giant dunes – frantically cleaning our weapons to free them from the all-pervading sand – we watched helplessly as several amphibious vehicles that had made it safely ashore and were trying to find a way through the dunes blew up on mines, their tracks digging deep down into the sand and exposing the explosives which had allowed the first in line to pass over safely but had blown up the ones following. These burnt furiously and in one dreadful moment two of the mined amphibians burst into immediate and quite unapproachable flames with no chance of anyone being saved, while yet another struck an enormous shell laid as a mine, killing its eighteen passengers.

We started our attack on the coastal battery immediately to our front with 3 Section leading. We shot the defenders of its command post and hurled grenades into its large concrete pillbox defending it, and then disaster struck. Mortar bombs suddenly deluged the whole of our troop's forward position; it was now afternoon and we had strayed into a killing zone. All our officers and senior NCOS were killed and others were wounded and incapacitated. Steve our Bren gunner who had an appalling stammer came to our rescue with a fine and accurate long-range shoot that silenced the enemy mortar that had caused all that damage and killed its crew. This mortar strike had fallen on one of the prepared fire zones where our enemy calculated we might stray into, and we did. Something very similar occurred later in Holland where a stretch of flat scrub some 50 yards square had been cleared to resemble a reasonable substitute parade ground. No self respecting Royal Marine officer of that period could resist a parade ground and this piece of ground admirably suited our new commanding officer's resented injunction for early morning assembly, complete with polished cap badges extremely brightly polished boots and prolonged physical exercises to follow, despite the presence of our enemy 300 yards away across the River Maas with his mortar position quite close behind, which promptly distributed 30 bombs across the parade ground. This pestilential figure with giant ego and a brain that could easily be accommodated in a very small aspirin bottle was not with us for long but was exceedingly troublesome while he was.

Along with the rest of the troop, 3 Section surged along the awful dunes and raced into the concrete gun emplacement attached to the nearby main coastal battery. One of our number fell but after we had thrown a couple of grenades it was clear the garrison had little taste for mixing it with us and they surrendered. Out they came with a white flag and their hands up, some 30 men surprisingly large and fit looking, while another larger group of supporting infantry fought to the last, despite being offered surrender – these were recent arrivals who had been withdrawn from the Russian Front. Once more our weapons fell silent, full of drifting sand. We were in any case very short of ammunition, not to mention cold and hungry on the exposed dunes.

I was sent back from this forward position as night fell to help collect what food could be found and to inquire as to the whereabouts of ammunition supplies. It was a weird journey over a recent battlefield across desert, dune and marshland recently disturbed by a late afternoon intense bombardment by our own supporting forces for a change, including the exciting emergence of 20 or 30 Spitfires sporting 500lb bombs and assorted cannon fire.

While daylight lasted our own small mortars had made smoke for 3 Section and 100 other marines to stagger forward across what seemed an almost endless stretch of barbed wire protecting yet another battery and its secondary slightly smaller gun position. We had thrown grenades on dangerously short four second fuses and shot or bayoneted its defenders. Alistair McGonegal used his Commando dagger, a large, long, heavy knife to gruesome effect. I felt as close to vomiting and despair as I ever did or have done since. As we left the casemate a German officer threw a stick grenade; it landed at my feet and didn't explode. I shot him twice and he fell to the ground with a smile on his face.

As I crossed the gloomy desert-like terrain heading towards the beach area, hoping to find food and ammunition, I came across the sad debris of recent fighting. I saw a dead Commando and a few yards further on a dead German, both in almost the exact same position as if they had shot each other at the same time. Our medical officer and his orderly were lying with bandages still in their hands, killed by a mortar bomb as they dressed the wounds of their friends. At one point a ghastly simultaneous bayoneting appeared to have taken place. When I reached the beach I discovered that ammunition had already been sent up to the forward positions. I scrounged two Cadbury's fruit and nut chocolate bars.

When morning came, and with it miserable cold rain, we attacked the remaining battery after a major seaborne bombardment from our supporting battleship HMS *Warspite*. 3 Section had two of its members wounded including our amateur barber who had given us a thorough shearing before the battle for which he claimed we hadn't paid him. He was hit in the hand, which didn't look too good for future haircuts. We took well over 100 prisoners, secured the surrounding dunes and a nearby village, which was the first habitation we had seen in two days. Here we caught a sniper in the small church bell tower and shot him; we left him hanging athwart the big base bell.

Well into the second day of non-stop drama combined with a good deal of fear and trembling we made way for the Commando which had been held in reserve. Its Colonel, an irascible peppery sort of chap, had kept on trying to force his men through our positions to take on the enemy – we supposed in search of glory. After two days he succeeded much to our annoyance and great inconvenience. This unit then made a bad mistake in trying to take on a battery and its defences untouched by bombardment and still fighting hard, so back they came in disarray and foul temper. We had to provide a troop of our own men together with a full assortment of our own and captured enemy machine guns, and the terrific supporting fire these put down flattened any serious attempt at resistance and enabled the other Commando to take the offending battery by storm at the second attempt. 3 Section tried to help by laying smoke from our small mortars and clapped some of them on their way back from their successful assault, which wasn't appreciated and a complaint was made. Their Colonel and ours apparently had a lively discussion on this matter and agreed to differ; the offending Commando remained a thorn in our flesh for sometime after but both Colonels became Generals.

After the fighting was finally over with the entire German garrison killed, wounded or captured we took part in a thanksgiving service in a small local church sparsely attended by us but enjoyed by many village and townspeople who turned out in full national costume. We then removed ourselves to Holland still very much on a war footing and at once prepared for further dramatic surprises. As a less than dramatic postscript the Marines on board our supporting battleship who had bombarded splendidly if a good many miles offshore were awarded 21 days homecoming leave when their ship arrived back in England; ah well!

Having written at some length about the efforts of our fighting troops it would be very unfair not to mention our support and heavy weapon colleagues, those idiosyncratic, splendidly esoteric individuals who fired our Vickers medium machine guns and the mortars. The mortar section landed safely in the first wave and was established behind a sand dune around which large shells were landing, bringing their weapons into action within fifteen minutes.

Their radio connection was badly affected by the blowing sand which put them out of touch with their fire controllers and the difficult carrying of weapons and ammunition across the infernal sand of the dunes compounded their problems, but they not only managed to support us but were able to fire frequent shoots in support of a struggling neighbouring unit. Our machine-gunners in the second assaulting wave were in desperate trouble from the start and only managed to bring ashore two tripods and a small clearing plug. Trying to keep us all in touch with each other were our signallers manning some sixteen sets of varying power and effectiveness. Five signallers were wounded on the first day and several radio sets were lost on landing; brigade headquarters, surrounded as they were by burning amphibious vehicles, was lost for the whole of the vital first two days. At one time the signallers had to resort to semaphore in short hand signals. It was a Royal Marine signaller who saved an amphibian and its crew by hurling all the burning equipment overboard and he was awarded the Military Medal. Enemy shelling and mines on a very dangerous beachhead complicated the task of administrating the Commando.

The officer in charge was mortally wounded on landing, and later a gale prevented stores from being landed and a Herculean daily two-mile journey across the dunes had to be made many times carrying food and ammunition. A path was eventually constructed for amphibian vehicle use though only six out of the original 22 remained in use after the second day. The food shortage was only relieved by the discovery of a large store of German food.

There was surprisingly no enormous resentment by the population to the breaching of the dykes and the flooding of the island and their homes; on balance it was felt that it was better to suffer the floods than continue to put up with the Germans.

So this unpleasant week came to an end. We had beaten 10,000 Germans with the enormous help of artillery provided by the Royal Navy, the Royal Air Force and fellow Royal Marines whose anti-aircraft guns defending Antwerp were successfully used in the role of ground artillery. There was never the slightest difference in terms of all-round excellence between an Army and a Royal Marine Commando. I served with both variations on the main theme; they all shared the same ethos, did their basic training at the same camp in the Scottish Highlands and all suffered from the difficulties that camp had in supplying men to the sixteen Commandos who fought in north-west Europe, Sicily, Italy and out in Burma. If I had to find one word how Commandos stood out from their fellow infantry it would be resilience. Their training taught them nay, absolutely insisted they always, unhesitatingly produced that extra 30 per cent of effort.

The Commandos engaged on Walcheren Island were numbers 41, 47 and 48 Royal Marines and 4 Army. 41 had fought at Sicily and in major battle in Italy. 47 had captured Port en Bessin in Normandy, designated as the main source of supply of petrol to the entire British and Canadian armies, and had fought the most epic battle of any single small unit in the entire war, according to General Horrocks in his post-war television broadcast. 48 was the youngest Commando of all, formed just three months before D-Day to fill a gap at the extreme end of the Allied line. It had been a woefully mismanaged Marine infantry battalion in Sicily but in proper hands from France to Germany in 1944–45 it became the best of the lot. 4 Army Commando with whom I spent three unforgettable months was the largest in the brigade at 800 strong, comprised of free French, Belgian, Polish and Norwegian troops and of course a famous Highland Piper who piped them ashore on D-Day. The casualties of our Commando at Walcheren were more than a third of all those who fought. On D-Day in Normandy they were not far off a half.

With our business in Normandy concluded I was told to prepare to return to England in order to attend a sniper's course. I was a natural rifle shot and looked forward to an entirely new experience. The means of transport was to be landing craft, setting off, as it turned out, from an adjacent stretch of beach to the one we had landed on back in June. The beach looked as if it had been raped and pillaged, still littered with debris and abandoned military hardware, and offshore the sunken merchant ships used as a breakwater to assist the endless landing of stores were still in place, storm-battered and forlorn. I had a long look around Langrune – the small town behind the beach surprisingly untouched by the D-Day naval bombardment – and I wondered where all the shells supposedly fired in our support could have landed. Certainly not on the enormous concrete strongpoint by the promenade which held up and repelled every attack made on it from eight in the morning until late in the afternoon.

I walked into the town and felt sure I had found the deep trench from which the unfortunate coastal defence Germans had, far too late, tried so hard to surrender. Just behind it was the fortified house from where I had seen the enemy sniper leaning out of the top window to shoot two of our accompanying Canadians as they battered away to break open the barricaded front door. It was lunchtime and, chomping away on some ship's biscuit found in an abandoned tin on the beach, I walked back to our intended site of embarkation and awaited events. The plan was to hitch a lift from a flotilla of small 11-ton landing craft of a type I knew well from early days in training. They were called LCMs or landing craft mechanised – diesel engined, flat bottomed and not much fun in rough weather. Just along the beach I could see a flotilla of similar craft in some disarray, but about whose fate and terrible problems no news filtered through until much later. However, I include an account of their travails because it was a very sad event and I had met and become friends with many of their Marines on earlier training exercises.

The Marines manning this flotilla had sailed independently in their small craft for the Normandy beachhead, a distance of over 80 miles navigating along one of the channels specially swept of mines for the purpose. Their passage was difficult – two craft had been lost on the way over and another on nearing Normandy – and it was a marvel that they reached their appointed place on the beaches. Here they were bombed and machine-gunned in hit and run air attacks night and day for weeks, and with only brief intervals for rest were engaged in bringing ashore every conceivable type of stores and equipment. Another eight of their craft were lost in the storms, which caused havoc in the whole assault area soon after D-Day. It was finally decided to send this flotilla back to the UK and they awaited their sailing orders in the Gooseberry (harbour formed by sunken ships). There were fifteen craft stored and provisioned for the trip including extra jerry cans of petrol strapped to the deck. They left the beachhead in the early evening. They ran into fog and slowly deteriorating weather; the change was hardly perceptible, one moment the sea was calm with a rather heavy atmosphere, next the flotilla was battering against heavy turbulent seas in a thunderstorm with gale force winds from the northwest and torrential rain.

After some hours of this the seas became so rough that very little headway was being made although the engines were being used at full throttle and it was decided that a return to the beaches would have to be made; in addition their petrol supplies were becoming low. When all the craft were collected a course was set to return to the beachhead, but by now it was pitch dark and the craft became dispersed – only five made it back to the beach some fifteen hours after they had left. Soon after they had turned towards what they hoped was safety, one craft developed engine trouble and it was decided to take off the crew into another nearby. This was carried out but in doing so and due to the rough seas both craft came into violent contact with each other and the steering of one was damaged in such a way that it became unmanageable. The Flotilla Officer then came to their assistance and managed to take off both crews. The total number now on the rescuing craft was three officers and 29 other ranks. When the Flotilla Officer had completed taking the crew off the damaged craft it was dark and the rest of the flotilla was dispersed and battered and doing its best to return to the beach; some of them even tried to resume their journey across the Channel. It was then found that the heavily loaded rescuing craft was becoming sluggish and investigation revealed that this was due to a leak, which had developed and was allowing water to enter the aft ballast tank.

Every effort was made to stem the leak and pump out the water, but the craft became increasingly sluggish and was suddenly inundated and began to sink. It was now 9.30pm and the storm was still intense. At the time of the sinking everybody on board had some means of keeping afloat through one form of rather inadequate life belt or another, but several were overcome with seasickness. It was a cruel twist of fate that the craft having suffered from the battering it had received earlier then developed this fatal fault, which caused it to sink in such a very short space of time. It was not until first light on the following morning that the sole survivor was picked up; he was found in heavy low-lying mist floating in the path of a naval launch patrolling off the beachhead. Searches by sea and air were immediately put into operation but all to no avail. Of the 32 personnel who perished, the body of one Royal Marine was subsequently washed ashore in the Arromanche area.

We were about to board our allotted craft at about 2pm when a signal came through that because of severe storms in the Channel that had caused many smaller craft to sink in mid-journey, no further sailings were to take place of any small craft. They were to be loaded one at a time onto 100-ton tank landing craft and so another Marine and I piled into the otherwise deserted well deck of a battered old LCM which was then hoisted and installed.

It took us 22 hours to cover the 80 miles of the Channel; we had no light, no warmth and no protection at all from the weather, which was very unpleasant as it rained heavily most of the time. To add to the general feeling that no good was likely to come of all this, moorings attaching us to the larger craft came adrift and for a desperate half hour we thought we must surely be pitched over the low sides of our host craft. Finally we made contact with one of the sailors manning the tank landing craft; he told us they all thought that our smaller craft was empty. Before sailing we had been ordered never to leave our LCM unbidden, however our new friend invited us to the gallery to have some breakfast, at which point we had been aboard unnoticed for 17 hours. Breakfast and some cheery company went down splendidly and we were relieved to find we were now in relative calm. The storm having been so severe our captain had decided further progress was impossible and we were now hove to in mid-channel. Some five hours later we sailed down Southampton Water in brilliant sunshine, pausing only to listen to George Formby playing and singing to his banjo, 'When I'm Cleaning Windows', he and his formidable wife Beryl being aboard a large landing craft on their way to entertain some troops in Normandy.

Our unpleasant journey came to an end at Westcliffe-on-Sea in Essex, where I learnt that my sniper course down in Wales had been cancelled. A week later I was on a large tank landing ship being gently swayed to and fro on my way back to France where we landed at Le Havre. I hitched a lift in a lorry belonging to the South Staffordshire Regiment almost as far as the Commando's new position close to the Belgian border: well, I did have to walk the last 20 miles. When I finally arrived I was greeted by our Sergeant Major.

'Where the hell have you been?' he shouted.

'I've been to sea Sergeant Major' I told him.

8

1945: Holland

A surplus of horror demands a surplus of humour. Especially in wartime.

Out of what had been a clear blue sky a good deal of rain was now falling. It was February and we had moved into Holland. One midmorning Fred and I were crawling on our hands and knees across some Dutch sand dunes, damp, gritty and altogether unpleasant. Our rifles were ridged with sand and unworkable, though this mattered little as we only had blank ammunition to fire at a long line of coalscuttle-helmeted Germans making their way slowly towards us. This was due to one of several recent cock-ups perpetrated by our Sergeant Major.

I looked over my shoulder down to a small beach but there was no sign of the landing craft we were hoping to rendezvous with. For no obvious reason I thought of my school days, also rather bleak but not life threatening, and wondered why on earth I had run away to become a Commando.

'Ere who was the bloke you said used to march on his stomach?'

'Napoleon,' I said, 'but it was an army he said marched on its stomach, it wasn't his own stomach he had in mind.'

'Well, I wish he was bloomin' well 'ere now and we could all 'ave a blooming good crawl together.'

A long burst of machine-gun fire ripped passed and ricocheted off the wall of an abandoned pillbox. We hurled ourselves out of sight and stumbled, engulfed in sand, down to the small strip of beach. Sheltering by the seawall we found the rest of 3 Section and made our way to a line of rocks 200 yards away where we could just see a small landing craft swaying to and fro in the sea. A clutch of mortar bombs landed with a loud shriek about a cricket pitch distance away, showering us with wet sand and pebbles.

We reached our craft and rolled over its side; the coxswain manoeuvred us round the nearby headland before we started back towards the mainland and safety. However, an enemy machine gun continued firing and its final burst caught Ted Allsop, threw him violently off the stern where he had been hauling in the small anchor, and he fell with a crash into the boat. He lay on his back with blood all over his stomach and died on the way back. Ted had been a Durham miner; his mine ran under the sea and he used to explain its workings in much detail. More excitingly, he believed he had an operatic tenor voice. It was certainly a very loud voice and any glass or fine bone china that came within striking distance of Ted in full vocal vigour would have known all about it. He accompanied himself with fine operatic gestures too and his face marked throughout with black and blue specs of coal, was full of intense dramatic expression not always in kilter with the subject of his song, his being a very fierce warlike face. His favourite song was a melodramatic affair called 'Jezebel', which required a final note of such length and intensity it quite terrified his audience and once even reduced Ted to tears. Dramatic art, he used to call it, and quite rightly so.

When we arrived back at our jetty we were met by the Sergeant Major.

'Your cap badges are dirty.'

'We shouldn't be wearing the bloomin' things on patrol, anyway' was Fred's sensible reply. Later on our cooks served up an insipid meal of stew. 'Did you know' Fred asked them, 'that an army marches on its stomach?' They said they had heard the saying.

'Well,' Fred told them, 'any bloomin' army you cook for wouldn't get blooming' far!'

It was decided to raid fortified German positions about 40 minutes journey by landing craft off the Dutch coast. It was hard for the ordinary Marine to see why this was a good idea. A major battle had just been fought to clear the approaches to the port of Antwerp, when a Commando brigade 2500-strong defeated almost 10,000 defenders. That was understood as a strategic necessity and a fine tactical triumph, but some of us felt that for smaller occasions a live and let live policy was a good idea. However this was not to be and a troop attack of some 70 men, reinforced to a total involvement well in excess of that figure, was organised.

We were told to travel as lightly equipped as possible; this is what I carried:

Rifle and bayonet with full magazine of five rounds
Two heavy iron hand grenades, perhaps 3lbs each
Two phosphorus grenades, of 2lbs each
Four spare Bren gun magazines made of metal, holding 100 rounds
Two canvas bandoliers of rifle ammunition, 100 rounds
A pistol and its bullets I had found and decided to take along (not issue), say 4lbs
Six PIAT bombs at 2.5lbs each
A full water bottle
Entrenching tool and handle

Throw in the boots I was wearing and the total weight was slightly over 69lbs.

We spent several days in rehearsal and briefing. We were shown photographs of barbed wire we might encounter both before and after the RAF had bombed it. When we arrived on the scene we found it still as it had been 'before'. Where they had taken the 'after' pictures goodness only knows. Our RAMC orderly who I think was a pacifist brought us up to date with first aid. He wore thick glasses, refused to carry a personal weapon, laughed a lot and had

won the Military Medal for rescuing wounded on D-Day. I practised with my newly found pistol and wondered how on earth one
hit anything with it, so great was its recoil.

We set sail at 10pm in several assault landing craft each holding
30 men in complete darkness and bitterly cold weather. Two hours
later we were back where we started due to engine failure and
a faulty compass. The next night was more successful. We landed
unopposed on a large dyke and at once came across a deep minefield 200–300 yards in length. We ran out of marking tape and this
gave us enormous trouble. Nine of us became minefield casualties
made worse by rescue attempts when others fell victim as they also
stood on mines. The wounded lay in wretched straits for almost
five hours attended only on a first aid basis until their return to
the mainland became possible. At the end of the minefield was an
extensive barbed wire defensive system in front of a large concrete
strongpoint protected by a system of trenches, machine guns, rifles
and hand grenades. White magnesium flares lit the area as bright as
day.

I had unwillingly become a permanent member of the 'throw
yourself flat on the barbed wire and let everyone else run over
you' party, a terrifying occupation when you consider that the
wire often had explosive charges attached to it. The wire was very
strong with large barbs wound on to it at frequent intervals and it
was often actually sewn into the ground in case you thought to
crawl through or round it. In addition I had to find somewhere to
park my bombs and retrieve them after the assault in which I was
expected to take part. All this in the inky blackness of a moonless
night one minute and the next second brilliantly lit up by flares
for all to see.

In an effort to destroy the barbed wire a Bangalore torpedo was
used – essentially a long hollow iron pipe with a fuse attached
and stuffed with explosives. This was tucked into the wire by the
aptly named Marine Mole, who led a charmed disciplinary life,
always questioning orders and refusing to call officers sir, insisting
on addressing them by their first or second names. For his efforts

with the Bangalore torpedo he was given the choice between a 21st Army Group certificate to be presented by Field Marshal Montgomery, or a two-week sniper course in the UK. He sensibly chose the latter.

Now came my big moment, and along with several other unfortunates including Fred who, at five feet five inches tall didn't cover a great deal of wire, I hurled myself at the wretched stuff with both hands over my face. Mole's torpedo, though it put him in danger and made a terrific bang, had not done a great deal to remove the wire. Having been well and truly flattened by my friends from 3 Section in transit over me, I untangled myself and in muscular spasm and mental shock I staggered vaguely forward towards the enemy strongpoint. Several hand grenades landed unpleasantly close and there was the bowel-loosening rasp and tearing sound of the enemy machine guns. I tripped over Steve our Bren gunner and gave him my four spare magazines. He swore at me and continued firing. Quite suddenly it all went quiet. The Troop Major and the Sergeant had made a medal-winning final charge, spraying the pill-box with their Tommy guns through its apertures and killing its garrison except for two frightened souls who were taken prisoner. Half a dozen enemy manning a supporting trench were fired at, two were seen to drop and the others made off into the night.

3 Section reassembled largely unhurt and we were told to patrol half a mile inland as flank guard protecting our main body, who were frantically engaged in the rescue and care of the minefield casualties. We took up a position by some lock gates where the Dutch gatekeeper told us a German patrol was due shortly on their usual inspection tour. Fred and I were in a nice cosy ditch beside one of the gates. It had begun to snow and I fell asleep. I woke to a shattering bang close to my right ear and a very large body fell on top of me. In front and above me was Fred looking at me with an expression in which blame and triumph were nicely blended.

'Getting our 40 winks were we?' he said. The German patrol had arrived and Fred had shot its leading member just as the latter had been preparing to shoot me. Another fight started and although most of the enemy patrol disappeared along a dike, three were seen manning a trench just beyond the lock gates.

'I'm going to get them to surrender' Fred said, and he called out something that sounded like 'angly-hock' which he repeated several times. Surprisingly two of the three at once put their hands up and started to come forward while Fred went magisterially ahead to receive their surrender. The third German threw a grenade, presumably at Fred, but he slipped, the grenade fell short and killed the two who were anxious to surrender. Fred then shot German number three.

The Section now decided to beat a path back to the landing craft and disappeared in that direction. Our Lance Corporal urged Fred and me to hurry up, there being an urgent need to catch the tide upon which the evacuation of everyone depended. He told us to beware of mines. He said the way back had been discovered to be heavily mined. Fred gallantly stayed with me and offered to help carry my wretched PIAT bombs so, still heavily burdened, we set off. We had not gone 100 yards when in pitch dark we ran into an extensive barbed wired apron fence across our path. An enemy soldier appeared on the other side of the fence and tried to fire his sub machine gun at me. At the same time I tried to fire my rifle at him, but both weapons were jammed with sand and refused to fire. He then threw his weapon at me and struggled, knife in hand, to climb through the fence. Fred – who was just behind and watching – moved forward and shot him. We became firmly entangled in our efforts to break clear and so did the PIAT bombs. It seemed ridiculous at the time, and has done since, that we were unable to free those bombs but their heavy wooden boxes and long supporting straps completely defeated us and, after an awkward quarter of an hour attached to barbed wire for the second time that night, being lit up once again by powerful flares, fired on by questing machine guns and a heavy gun firing at long range which had just started up, we left the bombs as they were and hopped, skipped and jumped through the minefield to the landing craft. I still have the camouflage jacket I wore that night with the badly stitched repairs I made to it. I have often worn it at football matches at wet and windy Anfield. It was a practical replacement for the heavy overcoats we had landed with on D-Day.

Back at our landing craft we found the Sergeant Major on his own, apparently doing nothing.

'You two can go back to the main minefield and help the others' the unpleasant man commanded. There were at least 30 people already helping and getting in each other's way and Fred's reply was about right I thought.

'No Sergeant Major! You can go an 'elp them yer bleeding' self.' There was no reply and we rejoined the Section where we dug in for the night because we were almost certain to miss the tide; there being no sign of our casualties we settled down to await events. It was then we heard the sound of tank engines starting up, and shortly after the familiar screeching and grinding sound of their slow forward advance.

For the second time that night I went into spasm, my heart pounding away and threatening to leap into my mouth. Here were several tanks coming at us and I had left the PIAT bombs, our main defence against them, half a mile away hanging on a barbed wire fence, and here was the troop commander asking me if I had the bombs ready, safe and sound. I felt apprehensive and frightened but more than that I experienced guilt and shame – by far the overwhelming emotion. I suggested to Fred that we make a last minute attempt at retrieval but it was clearly impractical. I talked it over with Bill, the PIAT gunner, who surprisingly was not too upset. We still had one bomb on the gun. I told the troop commander that everything was in order.

The tanks were coming closer by the minute and with them would come infantry and probably guns in support, but at that moment a miracle occurred. Our main radio – which had been faulty all evening – suddenly sprang to life and contact was made with our machine-gunners on the mainland and more urgently with our supporting 25-pounder guns. First came the Vickers machine guns firing their new long-range ammunition. We could see, in the now star-filled sky, their tracer bullets very high in a golden arc with their welcoming noise, which sounded partly like a skeletal rattle and partly the thunderous ripping of giant sheets of linen. Now came the reassuring whistle and shriek of artillery shells and the friendly crash and bang as they landed. Many thousands of bullets were fired and scores of shells. We heard no more from the tanks. Both they and any infantry were deterred or more likely destroyed.

The landing-craft commander gallantly reported he was prepared to risk another fifteen minutes on the tide, by which time the minefield casualties, all nine of them, arrived back and we set sail. One of the craft broke down at the narrowest point of the return passage and for several minutes we were fired on by enemy machine guns, but we were by now within range of our own mortars and our SOS produced an instant response. Well over 100 bombs fell exactly on the enemy position and wiped them out. We managed to set up a tow for the broken landing craft. I sat next to a sergeant from another Royal Marine unit who had accompanied us as a spectator to gain active service experience of offensive operations. I had been next to him on the way out when he was alert and eager for the action to start. Sadly he had been blinded by blast from a grenade.

We arrived back, the wounded on stretchers, shocked from their injuries and long exposure, our prisoners not looking too confident. We started to remove our black camouflage cream. A medical orderly preparing for the raid had confused his camouflage cream tube with another containing Gentian Violet ointment and, to the delight of his friends, went about with his face bright purple for almost a week.

Flying bombs flew overhead closely followed by anti-aircraft fire, we boiled out our rifles, submitted to the Sergeant Major's ridiculous early morning drill routines and marched off towards what we hoped would be a decent hot meal and sleep. By noon next day we had already spent several hours practising our snap-shooting on a range worked out and put up overnight and correcting mistakes made while laying smoke from our phosphorus grenades during a previous raid.

I once read a book of reminiscences written in diary form by a former leader of commandos in which he describes a particular period of time when all was quiet and no military events worth mentioning occurred. He made it sound like an amalgam of a minor bar brawl and a day out at the sales. I found in my rough notes of the same period, if in a different place, the following brief excitements covering one fortnight.

> Dusty Miller brings down Spitfire attacking same target as his mortar, pilot swears horribly at Dusty from his perch in tall tree.
> My friend Fred on open arrest for swearing at the Queen of Holland.
> Me to attend court of enquiry into illegal consumption of Iron Ration. 3 Section decide to shoot their sergeant major. Dusty almost manages repeat performance on some RAF fighter-bombers.
> Dusty blows up troop headquarters in demonstration shoot.
> All quiet in the Western Front?

Dusty's demonstration shoot came about over problems with the Corps' ammunition dump. The Germans had made two brilliant raids by sea along the Dutch coast when they blew up a large chunk of this vast store supplying ammunition to British, Canadian and Polish troops some 40 miles away on the German border. Defending battalions didn't seem to get the hang of it at all and their counter mortar fire served only to blow up those parts of the dump the enemy hadn't managed to hit. It was decided therefore to organise a competitive mortar shoot to raise standards all round, with a prize to the winners of a long weekend in Paris once hostilities permitted. The mortars under scrutiny fired 4 or 5lb bombs from heavy metal cylinders supported by clamps and brackets and were operated via higher mathematics by the more idiosyncratic members of a unit at an effective range of half a mile or so.

Our Commando was no stranger to the Corps' ammunition dump – in fact we had recently set fire to it during a training exercise and had not expected an invitation to the competition. However someone dropped out and our team replaced them. Dusty Miller was our star turn at six foot three inches with arms which almost seemed to touch the ground – a troop of orangutans had they been passing would have accepted him as one of their own, no questions asked. He could fire well-aimed bombs at the prodigious rate of over 30 a minute. I suppose rather less than 30 bombs would have been safer and possibly more accurate but Dusty had a marvellous record fully meriting the praise he received, even if his friends felt great relief when he finished firing.

The plan for the competition was for the mortars to fire just ahead of some advancing infantry who needed to show great trust and a good deal of courage. This part was to be played by 3 Section reinforced to some 20 unwilling souls. Eight teams were to take part. Despite a snowstorm Dusty started in fine form, hitting all his targets in quick time while whirling away like a demented windmill and easily overcoming all opposition. The semi-final was reached and that went well too, though Dusty blew up our starting hut as we left it. We arrived at the final to meet the favourites, veterans of almost every battle fought in the war so far.

To better view the proceedings, many distinguished spectators, some 50 in all including a fine posse of generals and even a passing visitor from the War Cabinet, gathered together quite close to the final targets in front of their many imposing looking vehicles. Dusty having obliterated all his targets in a state of mindless euphoria, continued firing, though his aim after shooting for so long had faltered and finally collapsed. He distributed several bombs close to 3 Section who fled the field. Several more bombs dropped excitingly close to a group of generals who easily beat any known record for the 100-yard dash and his final salvo hit both brigade and divisional wireless cars, several latrines set up for the occasion and the joint officers' mess. Surprisingly, no one was hurt except a lance corporal using the junior NCOs convenience who had some rather awkward splinters to deal with. At the court of enquiry Dusty claimed that he had sprained his wrist loading the final bombs and this explanation was more or less accepted but his further claim that he was entitled to the weekend in Paris was, some thought unfairly, turned down.

I should note that is possible in old newsreels to see pictures of these mortars being fired showing a single soldier strolling languidly up to his mortar, popping a bomb down it and then crouching, doubled-up, well away from it, with both hands pressed against his ears, then lighting a cigarette and gently repeating the process. Actual wartime firing was a whirlpool of skilled activity, not least to ensure that the bombs were loaded the correct way up. The Germans used to fire their rather bigger bombs off small lorries or tracked vehicles in quickly repeatable batches of ten. They were called Nebelwerfers and many Allied soldiers thought them the most dreaded of all enemy weapons. Of course they didn't have the individual virtuosity of our Dusty Miller.

A few days later we moved inland and our troop of 60 men were sent to support another commando trying to capture a fortified gun position defended by three tanks dug in down behind a big hedgerow. We took no active part in the struggle that followed, illustrating how often one is no more than a spectator of dramatic events unfolding a short distance away, in this case not more than a few hundred yards.

The attacking commando was supported at a distance by two 25-pounder guns and their own assortment of light machine guns, perhaps a dozen in all. But they got nowhere after attempting to overturn the opposing tanks and infantry. In mid-afternoon they managed to call up three or four fighter-bombers by radio and events started to go their way. But, although the gun emplacement was battered into bits and pieces, the defending tanks hidden in ditch and hedgerow defeated all efforts to get at them and kept firing away, exacting numerous casualties amongst the attacking troops who were fed up and vulnerable. But just as evening drew in and we were reluctantly prepared to join the fight, two of the three remaining tanks caught fire and one of them blew up. There was a pause and the crew of the last tank scrambled down and rather cocksure came forward to surrender, but their luck had run out. The leading troop of the commando, who had suffered most from hours of shelling and seeing friends killed and injured throughout the afternoon, refused their surrender and shot or bayoneted them, which brought the action to an end.

It came as a complete surprise when we were told to provide a Guard of Honour for Wilhelmina, Queen of the Netherlands. No reason for this was given nor any asked. We were relieved to get away from our problems along the River Maas. At dawn one morning and still in the filthy, lousy clothes we were wearing, we were bundled into lorries and driven for two bumpy hours and decanted into a large muddy field in pouring rain alongside a rural railway station without any identification. Three hours later we filled up with soup from a field kitchen, which had arrived –which served nothing but soup. Another hour went by and a field quartermaster arrived and we were issued with a full set of clean new clothing and a flannel each to wipe our mud-stained faces. A total of 400 mugs of soup, 400 sets of clean clothing, 400 face flannels and the return of the field kitchen with yet more soup and a ship's biscuit which proved too hard to eat even when laid out to soak in the everlasting rain, were issued. We then lined up on both platforms of the station and on either side of the swing gates marking the station approach 50 yards away.

In mid-afternoon, perhaps six hours after our arrival we were told that the Queen's train had been delayed, it was rumoured, by a halt for lunch. Shortly after as it began to grow dark we heard a train whistle down the line and could see a distant puff of smoke. We fell in as smartly as the squelching mud would allow and, well in advance of the train's arrival, we fixed bayonets and presented arms, while some well meaning but misinformed person tied a French flag to a nearby signal.

The train slowed down at the entrance to the station and a very ancient lady looked crossly out of the window.

'There's the silly old bag at last,' Fred called out and a military policeman standing by tapped him on the shoulder and took his name and number. Perhaps she heard him for the train instantly accelerated and shot away without stopping and the Commando was left presenting arms to itself across both platforms.

The field kitchen put in a repeat appearance and again filled us up with soup and then along came the field quartermaster's circus, who insisted we return all our nice new uniforms, underwear and face flannels, though threats of strike action and the efforts of a last minute deputation succeeded in permission being given for us to keep our clean socks though nothing else. We were back in the line, safe and sound and full of soup the same evening.

We were amazed and dismayed a few days after our efforts on behalf of Queen Wilhelmina that the whole Commando was again asked to become involved in what almost amounted to a royal inspection when a fierce little Lieutenant General came out to us in Holland to say goodbye. We had never met nor heard of him so we were really combining hello and goodbye and after he had gone – good riddance! There were no new uniforms and no soup kitchen, and our peppery little bantam of a general was not tremendously welcome and nor were the several miles we had to march in heavy rain to greet him.

He marched at great speed onto a makeshift parade ground and presented himself and his very large red nose in front of me as our unit right marker. Being the tallest on parade I was always the right hand man in the front rank on whom everyone judged their correct line and dressing and I was always the first available for inspection. The General looked up at me and said 'How tall are you, son?'

I was tempted to reply, 'Six foot four, dad' but just said, 'quite tall, sir.'

'But how tall?'

'Reasonably tall, sir, over six feet.'

'I bet you've never slept in a hammock' he said accusingly.

'Yes, I have, sir' I responded.

'You must have been very uncomfortable.'

'I was very comfortable, sir' I lied.

'I don't believe you,' he said, 'did you know I used to be a bugle boy?' I told him I didn't know. 'Well, I did,' he said 'What's your demob number?' he asked.

'46 sir,' I replied.

'Aha, mine's number one' he said triumphantly and popped off in delight, presumably to celebrate because he never carried out the rest of his inspection. After the General had vanished so did we, back to the line again.

There was a postscript to Fred's brush with the military police during our ceremonial labours, stoically endured, on behalf of Queen Wilhelmina. The MP concerned, along with the Corporal, paid an official visit to troop headquarters in search of a victim and requested an enquiry into Fred's conduct accusing him of 'hurling abuse at a royal person'. An enquiry of sorts was held, though most unwillingly, by the troop commander at which I was allowed a starring role as 'expert witness' being the only person present who could interpret Fred's speech reasonably fluently.

I gathered 3 Section together should they be required as fellow witnesses and we acted as fair counterweight to the Sergeant Major, who put in his usual appearance to make unkind and biased remarks about Fred. My case, such as it was, hinged on whether my word would be believed set against two unpleasant and unwelcome strangers. I called one character witness for Fred, Old Bill from Bolton, who made out Fred to be some kind of saint. Briefly, I said that Fred had not cursed, sworn or been in any way uncomplimentary to the Queen, on the contrary he had cheered her to the echo as all of us had tried to do until stopped by an unpatriotic military policeman. Our Major backed Fred entirely and the Sergeant Major, along with the police duo, lost hands down and were sent packing. Fred slightly spoilt things by saying rather loudly as they left, 'She was a silly old bag all the same' but by then we had already won our case.

Military police were not much liked – in fact apart from their mothers I don't suppose anyone liked them. When standing at crossroads under shellfire directing traffic they were brave enough and there was a section that capably looked after rail movement at and around stations, but apart from isolated events and incidents in their favour they were resented and more often than not regarded as 'nasty bits of work'. Of course public relations hadn't been invented then and by now they may all have acquired hearts of gold.

At night we were involved in frequent fire fights with massed Bren guns and free use of captured German machine guns. We were very aggressive and by day we shot up everything in sight, using incendiary bullets fired into houses the other side of the river. When the enemy ran out, sometimes with fire extinguishers, they were easy targets. We fired at a group of enemy cyclists peddling calmly along a road, and with our long range ammunition we chased them for almost a mile. They couldn't understand where the bullets were coming from and visibly panicked, several fell into a ditch and we saw others drop as a result of our fire.

Some Poles we had relieved left behind four of their tanks, which had broken down and were incapable of movement. Their guns were still in working order and the Commando second in command, fresh from serving on a heavy cruiser, went from tank to tank firing away at the enemy across the river and then left for lunch at headquarters. The irritated enemy replied with a far heavier concentration of shell and mortar fire, putting the tanks completely out of action, together with Fred and me when our dugout collapsed burying us under a ton of earth and hundreds of flying splinters. Another unsuccessful enterprise was our attempt to train some Dutch and Belgian troops who were positioned on either of our flanks and who detested each other and often fought one another putting us at severe risk trying to separate them.

We were warned of an enemy attack from northern Holland and we felt repercussions from an offensive from the south. Patrol activity hotted up considerably and we were out day and night. The troops were involved in a desperate little fight, if short in duration. An ambush was intended using an old factory building on the riverbank. It turned out to be almost a re-run of an earlier tussle. We left two of our number in the building while the rest of us went forward to check the surrounding area. While we were away the enemy sprang their own ambush, attacking us both in and around the factory, which they set on fire. What is often referred to as a 'spirited fight' now took place, which frankly we lost. Three of us were badly wounded and had to be left behind and one Marine was missing. On the way back to our base we stopped to knock down a house from which an enemy machine gun had been firing. Grumpy Gough set up his PIAT gun to use it in a house-breaking role and opened fire. But a hitherto invisible enemy surfaced and in the ensuing fight, although we killed them, we had further casualties one of whom was poor Grumpy who became walking wounded with an awkward injury from a grenade splinter in his derriere. Darkness prevented us assessing enemy losses.

During a visit to the quartermaster in pursuit of new underwear I noticed a Colt 45 automatic pistol and a box of ammunition lying on the ground by the official tent used in our recent past for assembling face flannels and uniforms. I was last through the process, there was no one about and the quartermaster's staff had finished loading their lorry, so I pocketed the pistol and its bullets and made off with them. I did this because, being semi-permanently employed as carrier of the anti-tank PIAT bombs, I was unable to reach and use my personal weapon, my rifle. In short I could be shot at but couldn't fight back. All other specialists, the PIAT gunner himself, the Bren gunner, signallers and engineers carried pistols to get round this problem and, though I had asked for a pistol while employed on the PIAT, not to mention my job lying on barbed wire, my request was denied. I stole the pistol and felt a lot more confident.

I practised hard using it on a makeshift range but I never quite mastered the weapon's surprising kick or jump on firing; it was like a small piece of artillery. I tried it out at 25 yards holding it in one hand then in two hands and shot at five-yard intervals all the way down to five yards and I never once hit my target. Finally I tried again firing two shots at a time but still my accuracy hardly varied. It was very disappointing but I kept trying and I still, absurdly, felt better and safer for having it until one very early morning I had a two-hour stint on the section Bren gun. I used the short cut method of loading my pistol, intending to save one or two seconds, it went off with a loud report and the bullet went through my hand.

The Section tumbled out of the ruined cottage in which they were spending the night. They looked angry and alarmed but cheered up a bit when they saw the cause of the disturbance. 'It's only Lofty,' someone called out and most of them went back inside. I stayed outside, shocked, bleeding and dismayed, wondering when the pain would start up as it eventually did along with interesting discoloration – yellow, blue and black. The Sergeant Major appeared in his usual bullying and irascible form, no metamorphosis there.

'I might have guessed it would be you!' Old Bill from Bolton came to my aid and bound my hand with his own field dressing, a very rare event. Field dressings could be a wounded man's link to life as combined stauncher of blood and tourniquet, an intensely personal item of equipment, seldom lost or given away.

When I pointed this out to him he said, 'Don't worry, you can buy me a pint sometime.' Bill had been at the siege of Tobruk, invaded Sicily and fought in Italy and Normandy. He had been one of my minders when I joined the Commando; my artlessness had made him laugh. I was touched and grateful to him and still am. A jeep arrived and took me to a field dressing station a mile behind the line and from there an ambulance drove me the 33 miles to hospital at Tilburg. The driver was a Canadian, of Native American caste, who had fought on the Normandy beaches with a regiment called the Algonquin Highlanders. He regaled me with his story of how, not having a rifle or bayonet handy, he had stabbed his German opponent through the neck with a sharpened pencil.

I was in hospital for three weeks and read *The Pickwick Papers* for the first time. I shared the ward with Canadian soldiers; my next door neighbour had been hit by a machine-gun bullet and lay in bed with a permanent drip in him and a sad smile on his face – he appeared to turn blue and grey alternatively. Another had lost his leg but couldn't believe he had, felt sure it was still there, and kept calling out for his mother. Others were convalescent and randy and one of them told the story of the hospital patient who asked the night nurse to give him a kiss. She refused but the patient kept asking her to change her mind and give him that kiss and she kept on saying no. Finally the patient said

'Oh nurse, you are a spoilsport, why won't you gave me a kiss?' The nurse replied,

'I shouldn't be in bed with you in the first place.'

Penicillin was administered for a week every four hours via enormously long old fashioned needles, very painful. After a few days it was quite hard to find a fresh part of the target. Throughout my stay I found the attitude of the medical staff bleak and uncompromising. Just before my discharge I looked at my medical notes at the end of the bed and against the wound category someone had written 'query self-inflicted wound'. Literally this was so but intentionally it most certainly was not and a host of troubles unfairly resulted from this assumption.

An ambulance ferried me back to 3 Section who had been training hard on how to fight alongside tanks, and the next morning I had to attend a court of enquiry into my shooting mishap, presided over by the troop commander. He was a major, a former army commando and much respected. Also present to give me the worst possible character reference was the Sergeant Major. The troop commander asked for a loading demonstration, all too commonly used, and believed me when I denied that I had done it on purpose and asked me if I would swear on the Bible that I was telling the truth. When he could not find an English Bible he asked if I objected to a Dutch one, which I didn't and the proceedings came to an end with a routine admonition and that I was told would be the end of the problem. My version of how I came across the pistol – following the battle – was accepted.

It came as a real and depressing shock to learn that the new colonel had decided to court martial me and I was placed under open arrest until the trial. I learned much later that his decision had little to do with me but was made 'pour decourager les autres' there having been a spate of off-duty accidents amongst the more exuberant members of the unit. One chap, pretending to be a knife throwing act in a circus, had recruited a friend as his target using his own commando dagger which had gone through his friend's arm. Someone else, playing at being a sheriff with his pistol, called out 'hands up or I'll shoot,' which by mistake, he did.

My court marshal verdict of seven days of field punishment number one – in short a prison sentence with hard labour attached – came about without debate or discussion in strict accord with the new man's requirements and with little evidence of judicial procedure. Before I had finished speaking for myself I was told to sit down. My defending officer doubled up very well as an assistant prosecutor and once again up popped the redoubtable Sergeant Major as a character assassin. I was then driven off to serve my sentence in a rat-infested dungeon, part of a ruined castle in Bergen op Zoom. The guards were uncouth louts of the Royal Marines Military Police.

My cell had one other occupant apart from the rats, a splendid chap called Joe from Wolverhampton, who turned out to have been a plumber-cum-joiner in a previous life. There were no beds or bunks in our cell, just a damp stone floor below ground level and a pile of ill-assorted wooden planks thrown at us by our guards. Joe made me a first class bed. It had no bedding but boasted a solid structure clear of the stones and rats. Joe was serving fourteen days for forgetting to come back off leave.

Our prison routine was much the same each day. We wore full marching order of perhaps 40lbs basic weight every single minute of the day, made up of belts, pouches, entrenching equipment, a large pack full of bricks and our rifles minus their firing mechanism. Brasses had to be polished as for royal inspection and our webbing, several acres of it, was scrubbed green one day and dazzling white the next. We had to run everywhere at all times. When occasionally given the command to halt we marked time at a fast quick step.

We did this for ten hours from seven in the morning to five at night when we started the polish and Blanco process, an allowance of twenty minutes being made for lunch and ten minutes for supper. When we ground to an unavoidable halt, we recovered our breath scrubbing floors and cleaning latrines. Once, while scrubbing away at the local brigadier's private staircase, the general came clumping along and asked the police corporal in charge,

'What's this man doing here?'

'Scrubbing these bloody steps,' I interjected.

'I'm not addressing my remarks to you, keep your mouth shut!' I did, and gradually the week came to an end. I said goodbye to Joe without whose cheery resilience it would all have been very difficult. A jeep arrived from Commando and an hour later we reached troop headquarters. I trudged a muddy mile to the forward positions and dropped into a damp hole alongside Fred.

If Fred had a fault, which I don't for a second think that he had, it would be that he snored louder than several hundred elephants. At night, dug into our small redoubt, I must have shaken Fred awake more times than I care to remember.

'Fred, you're snoring.'

'No. I'm not.'

'Yes, you are.'

'No, I'm not, I never snore.' All this with the enemy quite close at hand. I would look intently out at trees and bushes that always seemed to be on the move resembling Hitler Youth SS about to charge, but all would be quiet. Then Fred would start to snore again. I have always assumed we were spared disaster because our enemy never believed a human being capable of such a noise. The colonel visited us one very early morning while Fred was snoring at his loudest and he told him he was a menace to the unit's security and made him report sick. The medical officer gave him three nights off-duty to try out various remedies – the most sophisticated of which was putting a sock over his head – but it made no difference. Apart from attending to Fred, my first job on my return was to shoot two stray dogs as part of the latest batch of field regulations to prevent rabies.

We took over ill-dug and dirty positions constructed in the dike along the River Maas which was 150 yards or so wide and near the town of s-Hertogenbosch, the home of Dutch Advocaat production, where several important railway lines met and not long ago had been the focus of costly offensive operations. We relieved the Household Cavalry Regiment who patrolled a long front from the comfort of their armoured cars. Patrolling was our function here; there were three main varieties, all unpleasant.

One patrol acted as an early warning system, 50 yards in front of our wire, or if there was no wire, on its own, just ahead of a line of trip flares. Three men would stand for two hours at a time in a neatly dug slit trench too narrow to turn round in, not deep enough for a tall man, too deep for a short man and impossible for anyone with a large frame. The most disadvantaged was a tall man who remained in almost total silhouette, an especially unhappy situation on moonlit nights. The idea was that if an enemy came by he would see the three men in the trench and shoot at them, thereby warning the main position whose machine gun would open fire and finish off any survivors. This was called a night-standing patrol.

A second version of patrolling was investigative. Someone might report the presence of an enemy machine gun or mortar position. Out would go a patrol to look into the matter by day or by night using complicated compass bearings and esoteric map readings. No machine gun or mortar would be found but the patrol might get lost, ambushed and shot up. This was called a reconnaissance patrol.

Patrolling could also involve a really aggressive attempt to capture prisoners or a particular form of weaponry or just to create mayhem. Any number could take part in this not very cerebral activity, referred to as a fighting patrol.

A major problem when returning from our many night patrols was arriving safely without being shot by a sentry. It was hard enough to navigate the various hazards imposed by trip flares and your own minefields but worse still to find you had forgotten the password. If that was the case and the sentry was Alf Allday, your chances of a safe arrival were not good. Alf was a rarity, a Cornishman. He had helped his dad in his clock repair business, specialising in cuckoo clocks. He had an appalling stammer which he bravely surmounted by starting every sentence with the same short flurry of words on which further speech was balanced, they were 'I say look 'ere!'

Although in his early days with us he had to put up with jolly jests along the lines of, 'Come on don't take all day answering your name Allday', it wasn't until Alf kept turning up on sentry duty that his real problems started. He ably managed the formal barracks-style of challenge; in fact his hop, skip and a jump method prefaced 'Halt who goes there?' very well. But on active service, challenges got shorter and had to be done quickly and often, in the imminent presence of an enemy, very fast indeed. In fact there was no formal proclamation at all, just electric question and answer. The sentry under cover might say, very quietly, 'king' and would expect the correct reply in two seconds, 'queen'. If he didn't receive it he fired. This worked well until the arrival of Alf and the chaplain.

No one knew why the composition of the nightly challenge revolved around the chaplain but from then on it became elaborately scriptural. To have to reply to 'Jacob' with 'Esau' was one thing but when we moved on to 'Colossians' – 'Philippians' and 'Timothy' followed by 'Revelations' and then on one occasion 'Castor' and 'Pollux', we were all at sea, not least Alf. The suspense was enormous when events reached their challenging climax on the night of 'Jesus' to be followed by 'St Paul'. The chaplain, who happened to be passing, was shocked and surprised at hearing, 'I say, look 'ere Jesus,' from a nearby bush, forgot the reply and only saved himself by shouting, 'Don't shoot, good God, I'm your padre!' After that we went back to simpler challenges without Alf or the chaplain.

A few days later we attended a service in a small Dutch church. It was either that or help the cooks to construct a new cookhouse, so 50 of us filled one side while the locals sat on the other. We sang the hymns in English and they sang in Dutch – discord reigned.

Church services were popular before D-Day but much less so afterwards. A lot depended on the chaplains' efforts. To begin with we had an entertaining fire and brimstone chap who was heart and soul part of the unit, but he was badly wounded helping casualties and after that our moral and Christian fervour flagged a good deal. I think religion was regarded with suspicion and as its only representative was the chaplain, he needed to get its message across through being intimately involved in our activities and that included fighting and actively helping the fighting men. A very rough and probably inaccurate consensus was that the Roman Catholic chaplains best fulfilled this need. At any rate for our next action we had both denominations present.

We now had a very nasty battle to wade through during which we had to attack a large wood defended by German paratroops – the best defensive soldiers the enemy had. I don't believe after Crete in 1941 they dropped much by parachute but as conventional infantry they were high class, as good as we were and probably better fed. Some of their giant pots of stew we captured contained real beef and plenty of onions. They had a good cheese ration too.

Night patrols, street fighting and battling through forests were our most dreaded duties. Woods, full of cover with firebreaks giving a choice of natural trenches for the defenders, were high on our list of where we didn't want to be. The system of assault never varied wherever we were. Arrange for the guns to blow the place to bits and that would be it, all done and dusted, all we had to do then was to go peacefully ahead and 'put the kettle on'. In smashing up the battle area, of course, a fine series of defensive positions were created. A blown up ruin of a house has better cover than a standing one, a hole in the ground made by shellfire or a bomb is easier to defend than the flat space that preceded it.

We had a wretched time in that forest; we fought all day and never got past the initial line of inter-connected firebreak trenches. It wasn't until a flame-throwing detachment arrived that a decisive penetration was made. Watching the flamethrowers at work was surreal and awesome. We all felt desperately sad when it was finished, an appalling way of fighting, but got us into the wood and out the other side, where it turned out there had been relatively few defenders. Better reconnaissance might have saved us much blood, sweat and tears.

We ate the enemy's stew which we carried away in its giant pots and I found a letter from a newly married paratrooper telling his wife that he had managed to get a short leave to help with the expected baby. He was nineteen, he came from Duisburg and he was dead.

If that was almost the last fight with our real enemy, we still had the Sergeant Major to contend with and he was at his incompetent worst when he involved us in a midnight ambush on the Dutch and German border not too long before the final armistice. A message arrived from what proved to be an unreliable source that a last minute attempt would be made to parachute supplies to a German unit actively holding out quite close to us along a rural stretch of the River Maas. We thought to disregard this unlikely piece of news but the Sergeant Major became very excited at a chance to prove himself a latter day Napoleon and he made us gather in ambush in the middle of the night in a large field surrounded by steep hedges and lit by a reluctant moon. It started to rain and after a wait of some two hours several large pale shapes could dimly be seen floating into the field. Our military genius shrieked out, 'Parachute drop under way, Bren guns fire at will.' Four machine guns opened rapid fire and a bright white flare was sent up; in its brilliant glare could be seen no Germans, no parachutes and no supplies, just fourteen dead cows.

On occasional visits to Commando headquarters, it was always worthwhile to pop into the galley for a handful of raisins and then next door to the lair of the intelligence officer for tasty bits of information. A rummage round his desk in his absence always turned up something interesting. I once found an imposing document tied in pink ribbon and written in green ink marked 'secret'. It was from British 8th Army Intelligence in Rome and stamped on the outside were two words: 'Negative Bunching'. Inside it said that all infantry were to be told forthwith not to bunch together. It said this was definitely a bad thing though no reference was made as to where bunching was not to take place, it just told the local intelligence officer to tell the local infantry they would have to 'GIVE UP BUNCHING'. It could have been while lining up for their Sunday dinner. There must have been a missing page somewhere for that was the only reference. In the seemingly unlikely event that they were referring to battle conditions, this would have been a council of perfection as we all knew that bunching caused casualties and should never happen, but it did and would always occur because the poor old infantry feeling frightened, lost and lonely, reckoned their need for instant companionship to be greater than their risk of being hit by a hostile bullet: three cheers for bunching.

In an old biscuit tin was a miscellany of medals awaiting distribution. During the eleven months that the Commando was involved in non-stop fighting, 52 decorations of one sort or another were awarded. I think only nine went to Royal Marines, the rest going to officers and NCOs. I don't make any special comment on what tends to look a trifle disproportionate. Our first much respected Colonel used to play down over emphasis on an award of medals. He felt a bravery award and a particular act was perhaps not of the same value as daily stalwart behaviour and good cheer. As Fred put it, 'Monday's hero could be Tuesday's gibbering bloomin' wreck.'

Other excitements hot from our intelligence office featured briefings on the state of local enemy morale (good), the state of mind of recently captured prisoners (very annoyed), and a total misunderstanding of Marine Georges Beebe's report on an observation mission he had carried out due to 'Impenetrable dialect' (Huntingdonshire).

There was a report and stern comment on the casual burial of troops killed in small numbers, which had come from some distant echelon of command. This was deeply critical of the loss of identification tags and the leaving of the dead man's rifle upside down on the grave as a marker against permanent burial. The chaplain's department had got themselves into a fine old state over the planting of makeshift crosses on graves. Finally, on the subject of spontaneous burial, someone else was very worried that friends of the deceased should be leaving pleasant, family-style messages among these 'penny packets' of graves along country paths or in fields and hedgerows where they had fallen.

A grander scale of comment was made on subjects still exercising minds up to the present day. Who actually fired their weapons at the enemy? How close did soldiers get to their enemy? How to define a front line soldier and what proportion of the whole did he form? Another detailed form asked itself if it was safer to fight in a tank or to fire an artillery piece.

I was surprised to read of soldiers not shooting at their enemy by preference or specific intention. I do not believe that this would ever occur in a highly trained, motivated and aggressive unit such as a commando where basic training stipulated that everyone must give 100 per cent and then, without prior thought, another 30 per cent; reason had nothing to do with it.

While we were moving through northern Holland and over the border into Germany we came across two towns where there had been concentration camps, in fact both had been death camps. The first was quite a small place near a town called Oberhausen on the border between the two countries. As 3 Section passed by a camp we thought to have been already liberated and from which all prisoners had been helped away, we were fired on from one of the main buildings by some guards who were still there. We had no officer or NCO with us so we took matters into our own hands, hurling phosphorous grenades into the building from which the guards were firing and when it caught fire we shot them as they ran out. Across the border we arrived at the town of Recklinghausen at another camp where its guards were about to flee. We found scores of unfortunate men and women in varying degrees of wretchedness – some were barely alive skeletal figures, many were dead having quite recently been shot. The guards who carried out the killings were rewarded with litre bottles of vodka before and after each execution. We were about to shoot the 40 or so guards out of hand when the Colonel arrived and we had to take them prisoner. In the several days we ran the camp we made the lives of the guards as unpleasant as possible. We manned the four watch towers surrounding the camp parade ground and made the former guards parade on the hour, every hour and we fired machine-gun tracer bullets into the dust and gravel surface close to their feet to help them stay awake and keep the circulation going. It was done quite accurately with only a few being hit and exacted some small form of revenge if not justice for their crimes. We received a severe ticking off from several military bigwigs and were moved away.

It is worth mentioning that nearly every town we came across had its own version of a concentration camp where prisoners used for forced labour were set to work in the many nearby coal mines. When they were too sick to work they were shot. God alone knows what happened to the women and children. One of the visitors to this camp was a Captain in the Royal Engineers who was the sanitary inspector at Belsen in charge of putting that awful camp to rights. He was surprised to see how we were running our affairs.

Rather more than a year after all hostilities had come to an end in late spring of 1946, I was returning to England for demobilisation and I stayed overnight in a military transit camp at Nijmegen quite close to Arnhem, the scene of Montgomery's major faux pas and the demise of our former comrades in Normandy, the 6th Airborne Division, where I heard the most shocking story. It appeared that some 50 of our soldiers surrendered after several days of desperate fighting, being totally surrounded and without any sign of support and quite out of ammunition. After some delay they were herded into railway cattle trucks without food or water and just a single bucket for sanitation. They arrived at a camp in Germany where they were marched in single file in a tunnel and into a small courtyard where they were told to strip naked and herded into a large square chamber, like a con-crete box. To a man they all assumed they were at last going to have a shower but nothing happened. About half an hour later they were ordered back into the courtyard and as they returned a large cloud of lethal gas poured into the chamber they were leaving. They struggled back down the tunnel and were told by the guards to resume their filthy battle-stained clothing and they were marched away and taken out of the camp. An attempt to gas them all had failed through some technical defect. The long delay before the fault could be rectified allowed different orders to come through and they were all taken to another camp in eastern Germany where they were treated as normal prisoners of war. When the fighting ended and the war was over they made their way into Holland and finally reached the same transit camp I was to pass through a year later.

With regard to the question of the closeness of an enemy in combat, it was the opinion of one member of 3 Section that noth-ing was really close until you could hear your opponent belch and smell the onions he had eaten. I don't know any definition of a front line soldier. Fighting might have been safer in a tank, cer-tainly warmer, but far too warm if you had been in a Sherman tank under attack from a German Tiger. Better then to have been on foot and in a ditch, any ditch. On a battlefield, supervision and leadership was very hard to provide in the chaos and anarchy that soon replaced the calm of initial planning. Visibility was often lim-ited to a few yards, hearing became impossible over the explosive din, and it was far from easy to maintain intelligent thought let alone achieve tactical mastery of even a small fighting area. Chaos and anarchy about sums it up, which is why wars are won and battles mostly fought by small groups of men working together, three or four at a time across their battlefield, looking out for each other as they go and hoping for the best.

This was why our first Colonel was always appealing to his men never to let each other down, always to keep going together, never to take time off during a fight to light a cigarette and let their pals get on with the hard bits, eminently possible given the lack of supervision. He once put a notice on the board at Commando headquarters which read: 'In the day of battle everything turns, not as in a ship on the captain, but on the individual private solders.' A quotation, I think, from one of Sir Arthur Bryant's books but heavily underlined by the Colonel as follows: 'Never let down your friends however hard the battle!'

As I turned to leave the intelligence office on one visit I saw two small notices: one advised amphibious tank crews that in the event of their tank starting to sink they had 20 seconds to get out – an appallingly unfair balance of the odds, if unlikely to apply in the middle of Holland – and the second notice wanted volunteers to train as snipers. It reminded me of an unpleasant afternoon I had spent as one.

A serious professional sniper, fully trained and operational, is quite different to the chap perched in a tree or church tower. The former is more of a one-man army, tactically aware, mobile and equipped with all kinds of sophisticated help. One afternoon I was given the opportunity to try out this role when our despised Sergeant Major detailed me to relieve our regular sniper for a few hours. With no particular training, my only instructions being to shoot at any enemy target that presented itself, I was given a special rifle, complete with telescopic sight, and sent off to a nearby deserted barn. The barn was an old, ramshackle affair, its floorboards full of holes and the whole structure looking liable to collapse. Gingerly I climbed a rickety wooden ladder to the upper floor, crawled over to a window and poked the sniper's rifle through a broken pane.

Squinting through the telescopic sight I felt very unsettled. I was used to racehorse binoculars, but the degree of magnification here was of a quite different order. No matter how far away a tree, a stile or sheep was, it seemed to jump out and sit beside me. I was just wrapping myself around with straw and getting comfortable when without warning, the floorboards gave way beneath me and I fell clean through. Returning aloft via the flimsy ladder, no sooner had I located an alternative position than the same thing happened again. As I was picking myself up for the second time, the Sergeant Major arrived. He made his characteristically cheerless remarks about wondering why I'd ever joined up in the first place. I felt inclined to agree with him. After he left Fred arrived, who though managing to remain aloft, succeeded in putting his foot through the floorboards. Coming back down, the ladder collapsed under him, and off he went in search of another.

I was now feeling inclined to abandon the barn altogether, but when Fred returned proudly bearing a replacement ladder I decided to have one more go, and finding a third feasible sniping point, positioned the rifle and settled down to wait. This time I spotted a target quite quickly, a pair of German soldiers walking away in the opposite direction along a narrow trench. I followed their progress in close-up, and saw them halt by a hedge. Then, to my amazement, they set about using what appeared to be a latrine. As with the sheep and trees and stiles, I was astonished by how close the men appeared through the rifle sight; they could have been squatting next to me. A universal standing order from on high had decreed that we should kill three Germans a day. Well here I could fulfil two thirds of my quota in one go, or two shots, but I knew that I wasn't going to kill them. Why? A residual impulse from my schooldays about sportsmanship and fair play probably had something to do with it. Not that I had refrained from taking life prior to this moment, but the perceived proximity of these human beings was different to other situations, that and their vulnerability. Fred heard about it and laughed. The Sergeant Major also came to hear about it and spoke at length about his orders being disobeyed. On my way down the replacement ladder collapsed.

At dusk and sometimes at dawn everyone who was not manning a strongpoint, trench or ditch, used to gather together and flatten themselves on some smooth piece of ground at the rear of our position in a star formation thereby facing all points of the compass. I never entirely understood why this took place, though it was certainly chummy in what was often a frightening situation with the enemy a few hundred yards away. No conversation was allowed though quite a bit of sotto voce chat took place. Some of us for close comfort would move near to each other and link our ankles round those of our next door neighbour. I don't suppose our natural warriors felt a need for this but quite a few others did seek this comfort and I was certainly one of them. One night I felt Nutty Slack, our entrepreneur and 'black marketeer' usually so outspoken, brash and bold, curl his feet round mine and heard him very quietly say,'I am scared bloody stiff tonight, Lofty, how do you feel?' I said I felt exactly the same possibly even more so. 'That's a relief' he said,'I thought you was one of them brave blokes, here have some sweets!' and he handed me a week's supply of fine treacle toffee.

Some people may think of commandos as devil-may-care characters climbing 200-foot cliffs to get at their enemies with a dagger firmly clamped between their teeth and shouting wild war cries. If so they would have been very surprised to come across George Mulligan. Mulligan had been to an important grammar school and was an intelligent chap though so laid back in attitude he gave the impression of total disinterest, which annoyed all set in authority over him, sometimes very much so. He didn't look at all like a commando or a soldier of any kind, more resembling Billy Bunter, and he offended most basic military principles, notably that of punctuality. How he had come to be with a commando on active service was a mystery that never appeared to have been looked into. It was generally thought to have resulted from some major error in administration and in the mad rush of event s it was left at that.

Everyone concerned got used to Mulligan, officers and NCOs apart; he had many friends. His main point of dispute with authority, apart from extreme tardiness, was an unpopular habit of not so much disobeying orders but being inclined to want to discuss them first. He mostly limited this trait to requests likely to affect his own welfare, how far he was likely to march, for example, would there be a comfortable billet for the night, and he was always first to reply in some detail to the duty officer's routine mealtime inquiry for any complaints. In short he could be a complete pest to authority who tried hard to ignore him. His fellow soldiers found him entertaining and his grammar school status made him a great source of help in letter writing home or to girlfriends. A Mulligan letter to a girl brought an instant and often passionate reply. Several young men became unexpectedly engaged on the strength of a Mulligan letter.

Mulligan's day of destiny dawned as the Commando approached a line of small hills near the Dutch/German border; perhaps three large mounds might be a more accurate description. At any rate each mound or hill was protected by a concentric ring of defences including wire, bracken, thick gorse and several hundred German paratroopers, while each individual slope overlooked its neighbour. An initial bombardment by a field gun battery and three RAF Typhoon fighters was considered enough softening up and into the attack we all went.

We took the flat ground in front of the three hills though we had several fatal casualties in the process and a few more who were caught by the wretched wooden Schumines which tended to badly damage feet and ankles. The right hand or farthermost hill fell to a neat enfilading attack using massed captured German machine guns and, having taken at least a dozen casualties, we captured the central obstacle. However the defenders would not surrender. They poured heavy fire on us and we could move neither up nor down although as time went on and each attack failed it became obvious it was down we would need to go and that speedily. We were having maximum casualties from minimum cover and we had run out of momentum entirely. Defeat was literally minutes away.

At this point Mulligan popped up and quite without warning advised his troop commander that he had just remembered he'd been on a school holiday in the general area and better still could remember a picnic somewhere on the hill we were now struggling beneath. No one believed him because no one ever took Mulligan seriously, but he kept pressing his point until either through desperation or to keep him quiet Mulligan was told to take a section of eight or nine men along the route he was advocating and, complete with a machine gun, they set off leaving us with no great hope in our hearts and disappeared through an impenetrable mass of gorse and bramble.

Nothing was heard for what seemed an eternity although in reality it was probably only four or five minutes, when the sound of rifle fire and the welcome chugging noise of the Bren gun came down the hill along with the crack and bang of exploding grenades. This was followed by the triumphant return of Mulligan and his section waving a captured flag and pushing three German prisoners ahead of them. Thanks to Mulligan, whose pre-war school picnic site had turned out to be the top of the hill, the Section had come exactly upon the rear of the enemy position and, without any casualties to themselves, had killed, taken prisoner, or sent flying down the hill the greater part of the defending German force.

Everyone still standing, cheered, the officer commanding and several others were awarded gallantry medals while Mulligan received something called an Army Group Certificate and the promise of a weekend in Brussels or Paris when hostilities should permit. Mulligan chose Brussels because a trip from Germany would allow him longer there than Paris. He claimed he met Field Marshal Montgomery who gave him a Cuban cigar.

9

April 1945: Fighting Almost Finished

'We didn't know whether to shoot the Huns or the Officers.'
Private Soldier's Memoir 1914–18

Our Sergeant Major – as should be obvious from previous mentions of him – was a bully and a despot. He was an unintelligent tyrant who condemned and sneered his way through our lives, punishing normal high spirits with mindless severity and causing us more anxiety than the Germans. He wielded almost total power without sense, balance or fairness. He punished illegally, was tactically a second rate soldier, and was cowardly as well. It was his mean spirit that we found hardest to put up with, that and the shock and surprise that he existed at all.

His punishments involved serious overreaction without authority. He detailed Fred, who was five feet five inches and should never have been considered for this duty, as a permanent member of the 'spread yourself on the barbed wire' assault party, and myself at six feet four inches, who could cover quite a large slice of barbed wire, as carrier of the anti-tank bombs as well as other equipment. It simply ought not to have been done other than by rota. He was world champion too at minor punishments: extra drill at 3am on our way back from an all night fighting patrol, followed by a kit inspection. He had a quiver full of arbitrary punishments by night and day.

I am not suggesting that other sergeant majors were like this one, far from it. A good one positively swept problems away and could be the pivot for all progressive activity, as a lead and prime administrator. We used to think the best were overqualified as NCOs and should have been commissioned as captains or even in one case to major, but not ours.

We did gain one victory over this awful man. Marching back to billets across a sloping, muddy field, a large goat appeared through a distant hedge. It glared at us and immediately galloped to the charge, heading straight for us. The Sergeant Major yelled at us to hold our ranks and stand fast at all cost. He made such a noise that the surprised goat switched targets and went for him instead. The Sergeant Major fled, throwing himself on top of the nearest hedge, while the goat foolishly charged through underneath. We gathered round the fallen warrior and gave three hearty cheers – for the goat.

Events became so wretched and alarming we decided to shoot him. Fred and I drew the short straws and took the job on with no scruples at all, just an intense determination. We gave ourselves a fortnight to carry the project through – one way or the other. That it did not happen was not for want of trying, but of opportunity. He was very lucky to survive, but then he never appeared at the front on his own and he only once appeared in the lead. We were fighting at night at the time, which involved notoriously difficult snap shooting. We roamed freely in search of him, we manoeuvred and shot at him, Fred rolled a grenade into a dugout we had seen him go into during an attack but he vanished. We found him on his own at the end of a raid and could have nailed him there and then but there was no nearby enemy to explain away his body, no convenient gunfire or shelling. We had to leave him unharmed. It all became very risky but we kept on his trail until midnight on the fourteenth day when at the very last minute I saw him standing up some 200 yards away. I fired five shots from the hip in order to hide my silhouette as much as possible. I saw him fall but for whatever reason he had only gone to ground. I had missed and he lived on to plague us in exactly similar fashion for several more months. I was telling this story to a fellow Marine from another unit a year later in occupied Germany and he told me, 'We got rid of our bastard during a parachute drop. I put my boot through his chute.'

There was an interesting story about the crew of a mine-sweeper whose Captain had made their lives a misery on war service. They threw him overboard only to see him swimming back to the ship. Feeling guilty, they decided to take him back on board, which they did. From then until they reached port neither party mentioned the episode or behaved in any way out of the ordinary. Although the crew felt sure the whole matter would be reported on arrival not a single word was spoken and they all went their separate ways. I have no idea how often this extreme form of behaviour occurs, but in the case of front line troops, permanently scratchy, always on edge and threatened by death, it certainly can happen and long-term cowards and bullies need to beware.

There was a postscript to the saga of the Sergeant Major 30 years later when I took my dog down to the local golf club late one evening for a walk and a drink. There we came across a man I had seen in the bar before. He told me he had been wartime regimental sergeant major with a commando that had been in the same brigade as mine. I knew of his reputation as having been quite first class. He said he was employed selling cham-pagne, a correct occupation for an RSM I thought. Then he asked who my troop sergeant major had been. When I told him he expressed much pleasure and said if I wanted to look him up I would be pleased to know he was working a few miles away as a floorwalker at Burtons the tailors. I did not disillusion my new friend but I went along to the branch concerned and I stood at the entrance for a long time wondering if I should go in and tell him what we had thought of him, or perhaps greet him and shake his hand without mention of the past. I finally made up my mind and walked away.

As April arrived with snow and sleet showers so did an alarm call to fend off a series of brilliant German raids along the coast. Our troop's response was organised and surprisingly led by the Sergeant Major. We waited in ambush at selected points and towards evening in poor light saw a boat land a party 50 yards from us. We opened rapid fire but discovered we were using blank ammunition issued by the Sergeant Major. The presumably mystified Germans made off into the night, shooting at us as they went. No explanation was made that was in any way convincing.

We were in comfortable billets near a hamlet on the River Maas in Holland called Getruidenberg, following a long spell of fighting patrols and night raids on well-defended islands off the Dutch coast. We had just been deloused, had removed our fleas and applied the correct treatment for that other wretched itch, scabies, bathing in very hot water and scrubbing the many little marks until they bled. We were roused at dawn one day by a bugle call, unheard since our early days in barracks, and paraded fully armed outside in an early morning snowstorm. The Commando second in command with a supporting section had gone on a reconnoitring mission behind enemy lines and had not returned.

It was easy to lose oneself in the adjacent fenland area, not unlike the Norfolk Broad, full to the brim with narrow inter-crossing waterways but with few maps and, as no one knew where the lost patrol was and there had been no radio contact, it seemed an insoluble puzzle. However, we journeyed to and fro in our small flat-bottomed landing craft, jumping ashore whenever we saw the enemy and throughout the morning having a series of what military men called 'spirited fights' we dashed up and down endlessly steep dykes but we never sighted the missing patrol. We chased one group of Germans out of their well-dug position and ate their lunch of stew and goats cheese. We fought our way across a bridge defended by some twenty well-trained former Luftwaffe personnel. We failed to capture some strongly held factory buildings but set them on fire with tracer bullets and killed the defenders as they ran out, but still we saw no sign of the errant patrol. Then George Beeby got the chance to be a hero.

George had been a Huntingdonshire ploughboy. He had a wonderfully rich dialect, laughed a lot and told us endless stories, which he incorrectly believed to be funny. He would stand very close, look round confidentially and begin. When he finished he always smiled and said 'there, I thought you'd enjoy that little lot'. We always laughed, it was hard to avoid George and his awful stories but he was one of our natural warriors, enjoyed fighting and was very good at it.

That afternoon, walking along the bottom of a dyke, we heard sounds of battle coming towards us from the far side. I confess I hoped it would all pass on by and leave us alone, but not so George Beeby. When a stick grenade came flying over and actually landed at our feet he picked it up and hurled it back in one swift movement. We could hear the damage it did on its return journey quite clearly. A machine gun then fired at us from some rough cover to one side. We could see the German gunner busy trying to clear a stoppage on his weapon and so did Beeby, who promptly charged, yelling at the top of his voice while he sprayed the target with his sub machine gun. The German rolled away from his weapon and started to stand up to surrender but he was obliterated by Beeby's hail of bullets. That was worth any number of not very funny stories.

Then the thaw set in and it started to rain heavily. I thought of Fred and me sitting at the bottom of a steep rock face during our commando training in the Scottish Highlands, waiting for enough breath to return to fuel our further ascent when I heard him say, 'Bloody hell! They didn't tell us when we joined it was going to rain as well.' Well rain it did as we trudged along a narrow path leading into a large field bordering one of the many waterways where we expected a landing craft to collect and take us back to safety. There was no landing craft but we soon realised that we were being shelled slowly and methodically by a single German 88mm field gun. This was the most feared and successful artillery weapon used by any army during the war. There was no other gun so versatile and effective. Its nerve-shattering 'crack' and 'bang' resembled a super-charged bolt of thunder and lightning with its shells sometimes bursting just above your head and sometimes at your feet. In Normandy a small battle group of 50 or 60 men with a couple of these guns would hold an entire battalion at bay and like as not defeat it.

Why the gun's crew of four was bothering to direct the fire of such a super weapon to try and obliterate our small group standing in a field on their own without a warlike thought in their heads we had no idea, but pursue us round the field they did and round and round we had to go trying desperately to second-guess our opponents. We were stalked for over an hour in macabre and frightening fashion. We dreaded the crack of the gun and the sequence of explosion, black smoke and half a ton of mud and soil thrown into the air and landing closer to us each time. Almost twenty shells came our way and then suddenly that was the end of it, the gun ceased firing and all went quiet. I think it was the surprise, relief and elation that followed, which caused me to open my iron rations with all the trouble that ensured.

It was forbidden to open these small six-inch square bulky packs of emergency rations without the permission of an officer. None of us could remember that they had ever been opened though we always carried them. On one occasion we had no rations issued during two days and a night of fighting, unless one counts a couple of barley sugars every two hours, but nobody ever suggested we open our iron rations. In training we were taught *in extremis* how to chew on a length of cordite extracted from the metal casing of a rifle bullet and how to cope with the manic excess of energy this produced followed by vomiting and diarrhoea when the initial benefit receded, but no mention was ever made about the use of our iron rations.

At any rate in our euphoria at the end of eight days of awkward combat, not to mention our 4am start, and egged on by my friends, I gave way to a long felt curiosity to discover what was in my iron ration pack. When its loss was discovered at a later kit inspection, seven days of field punishment number two ensued. This entailed three hours of potato peeling at the end of each day and then two hours of night guard duty followed by one hour of sleep alternating for twelve hours throughout the night. Not too bad, though on reflection my voyage of discovery into the ration pack was hardly worthwhile. I remember an outer waterproof covering enclosing a hessian inner pack stamped in large purple letters 'August 1914'. The contents I recall were, a small chunky bar of plain cooking chocolate, another similar size bar of quite delicious fruit and nut chocolate, a cube of Oxo and a cube of Bovril. There may also have been two small matches and a couple of safety pins. I shared the chocolate with my friends but I was the only one awarded the field punishment.

About this time my friend Fred and I were elected our troop's representatives in a long running dispute with our two cooks who were not giving us enough to eat and certainly never offered second helpings. Providing that we could convince the Sergeant Major, we were told we might take our case before our troop commander, a Major, whom we trusted. Unfortunately he had a birthday and, hearing what was afoot, the cooks baked him an enormous cake and for the Sergeant Major an only slightly smaller one. We complained about this dastardly behaviour and the Major undertook to attend the daily mealtime inspection for a whole week to personally look into both quantity and quality of food on offer. His signing off verdict was that we were lucky to have such excellent and generous hearted cooks and considered our complaint to have been quite unjustified. He then went away and ate his cake and the Sergeant Major scoffed his while we returned to our previous helpings and slap-dash cookery, while the cooks continued, we suspected, to enrich themselves selling off surplus on the black market.

A tragedy occurred one Sunday lunchtime that underlined how wretched the behaviour of these cooks could be. Some 60 men were quietly queuing in their farmyard billet for their midday meal when there was a large explosion and an accompanying fire that killed nine Marines and injured several others. Cooking was managed by filling a long line of large iron pots with the intended ingredients, for example a meat and vegetable stew. A powerful flame was then pumped at high pressure under and along the line of pots with the one at the far end being sealed off. The cooks omitted this last vital precaution, the flame leapt the length of the pots and through the open end to where a trek cart containing a whole troop's reserve supply of at least a week's ammunition had been left close by unattended. Grenades, mortar bombs, shells and many thousands of rounds of ammunition all went up in a colossal explosion. There was never any official mention of this dreadful incident. We used to wonder how the letters of condolence to relatives and loved ones were composed. 'Your son was blown sky high waiting for his Sunday lunch.'

Three weeks before the armistice we were surprised to be issued with some splendid boots called 'Veldtschoen', intended for silent night patrols. They had intricate rubber treads and were so smart, so supple, so useful and overdue that everyone was delighted, but they only went up to size eleven and I took twelve. Determined to be part of the new fashion, I accepted the smaller size and went off on patrol in much discomfort. As we returned, just in front of our position, I stumbled and set a trip-flare off some 20 yards from the Section machine gun. We waited fearing the worst, not helped by our Corporal who had forgotten the password. We were vastly reassured when a familiar voice was heard to say, 'Come on in you daft beggars, I knew who you were, I could hear them bleedin' boots of yours squeakin' a mile off.' I handed my Veldtschoen back to the stores.

I think the Commando carried 50 spare pairs of ordinary boots in store somewhere. You handed in your regular ones for repair and drew a set of spares on a temporary basis. I had experienced trouble in earlier days when we paid an official visit to HMS *Victory*, Nelson's flagship at Trafalgar. The only footwear allowed while going round this ancient vessel was special lightweight 'sea-boots' issued for the occasion. I didn't want to miss out on an historic afternoon and accepted a pair two sizes too small. The six-mile march to and from the dockyard plus a long two hours aboard still rates high in my lists of agonising memories.

Our many fighting patrols and raids were our last warlike exploits apart, of course, from events surrounding the armistice. From then on we left the King's enemies alone. I think we were the only worthwhile, truly roadworthy infantry left in Holland. The others had all gone pell-mell across the Rhine several weeks before and left us fighting and bickering away on islands, waterways and riverbanks. Light aquatic infantry!

An armistice had been brewing up for some time and early in May 1945 someone in a distant echelon of command, replete with cigars, maps and brandy decided on a dummy run towards one. This was negotiated in fine trade union style and a triumphant communiqué was issued and read out to us in our holes and ditches. The enemy had promised not to shoot at us at night if we promised not to shoot at them during the day. At least that is my memory of it and the resulting confusion is very clear as well, though after several hectic days and nights, everyone ceased fire; well not quite. 3 Section didn't because of the Sergeant Major's insistence that we continue sending off 'Victory V' signs on the Bren gun. These were an admixture of Beethoven and government propaganda and quite hard to play on a machine gun. The Vickers machine-gun section also failed to stop, as did the mortar section and the Section containing captured enemy weapons who went on firing their stock of shells from an ancient but still useful French field gun. The 11am harassing shoot or 'hymn of hate', as it was sometimes called, had been going on for so long that no one thought to cancel it. It was extra special that day because the gunners decided to use up all their ammunition in one final fling. It was our biggest bombardment since and, some said, including D-Day and the Normandy landings, with every last bullet, shell and bomb fired away.

The RAF took a hand as well when 200 heavy bombers flew overhead to drop bread supplies on Rotterdam. An interesting mixture of bread and bullets, all administered under a flag of truce.

The Sergeant Major still had an irritating part to play. He reappeared with instructions to Fred and me that we go forward to accept the surrender of any enemy troops to our front. After all the recent crashing and banging we thought this very unwise and we scampered off to a flank well out of sight to settle down to a smoke and await events. Fred was on his second cigarette when something very surprising happened. From the ground opposite hundreds of men rose up out of their trenches and holes and instead of approaching us they streamed away across the fields in the opposite direction. They had all changed into civilian clothes. We assumed they were our Dutch SS opponents making off while they could.

We were wandering round the piles of uniforms and abandoned equipment when Fred called out, 'Come over 'ere quick!' I ran across to him ready for a last minute crisis and found him down a deep dugout, a crust of rye bread in one hand a chicken leg in the other, a bowl of stew steaming away on a small table and nearby a bottle of schnapps and two glasses. 'Come on' he said, 'let's fill our boots.' As we did a well-known lugubrious hatchet face filled the entrance to our dugout.

'You can't eat that stew,' said our dear senior NCO. 'It might be poisoned.'

'Oh, that's 'orite Sergeant Major,' said Fred, 'we'll take every precaution.'

'What do you mean you'll take every precaution?'

'Why, we'll give you the first bowlful of course!'

So that was the armistice, at any rate on our part of the front and two welcome changes came about. The Sergeant Major suddenly disappeared. I don't know where but he vanished entirely from the Commando and never came back. We hoped he'd gone to Burma. And in addition the pernickety, disliked, replacement Colonel retired from military service and went back to growing plums in Pershore.

10

1945–1946: Post Armistice and Germany

When our last bullet, shell and grenade had been hurled into Holland we were sent to Germany to bring as much calm as possible to that somewhat fraught place. We went by train; the journey took 21 hours and there was no heating and very little space. We mostly stood in the corridors, though the lucky ones snatched moments of relaxation on the luggage racks. Apart from a bar of chocolate each and an apple, no food arrived at all though we managed a brew-up using hot water from the engine which broke down several times as it coughed and spluttered its way through Holland and northern Germany. The nameplate said 'Herman Goering'.

When we arrived at Dortmund we saw a scene of complete devastation, repeated on later journeys through the Ruhr. I stood on the steps of what had been the town hall and calculated I could see an equivalent distance, had I been in London, from Piccadilly Circus to Hyde Park Corner, with not a single building standing even to first floor level. Everything was completely flattened and yet, less than three years later, I enjoyed steak and chips in a brand new three star hotel in Dusseldorf next to the rebuilt railway station and in Frankfurt I flew to London from a completely new airport terminal.

Our first billet in Germany was on the first floor of a small rural bakery opposite the local village inn where some of our unit had found a friendly refuge, at least until a notice went up declaring that 'No beer will be issued to any rank below sergeant'. Taking advantage of the lengthy meeting that then took place with the corporals, the rest of us helped ourselves until the taps ran dry. Nutty Slack, still in charge of our black market operations, acquired a large stock of bottled ale, which he refused to sell to sergeants and corporals unless the embargo on beer was lifted, which it was surprisingly quickly. We stood nightly guard in our bakery enjoying freshly baked bread at 5am each morning. Relations with a nearby winery were almost established but then we were posted far away from Dortmund.

We moved on to an enormous displaced persons camp containing 3500 men and women from eastern Germany and Poland and we acted as soldiers, police and often medical orderlies spraying disinfectant powder up and down shirts, skirts and trousers. We made dawn arrests of suspected criminals and carted them off to prison. We caught a gang who we suspected of having robbed a bank but wouldn't tell us where they had stashed the loot. Fred pointed a revolver at the head of the gang's leader and told him the first three clicks he heard would be from empty chambers, but he wouldn't hear the next one at all. The gangster revealed all after only one click.

After that we moved up to Westphalia to shoot deer and wild boar to help ease the acute food shortage in the Ruhr. At first we acted as beaters to drive game onto our machine guns but it made no sense to blow the beasts to bits so we were sent out as snipers and marksmen to live amongst the local foresters and farmers and in doing so we put a stop to widespread looting.

3 Section, now back to full strength of ten men, was rushed off to guard a famous art collection owned by the Prince of Arnenburg in a fifteenth-century castle in Kreis Buren. The Prince was looking after hundreds of paintings previously housed in bank vaults

throughout the Ruhr but threatened by the recent Allied bomb-ing. An attempt to attack the castle and rob it of its art collection had been made by Polish renegades from the nearby displaced per-sons camp and rumours were rife that other more sophisticated attempts were being planned, so we took up residence in the castle as sentries and armed guards. This was an entirely new experience, for none of the members of the section had never come across a castle before and we all enjoyed ourselves, as both the Prince and his Princess looked after us as welcome guests and in return we easily and decisively saw off the marauding Poles in true com-mando fashion – We shot the lot of them.

I had a jolly afternoon keeping goal for a team grandly called the 'British Liberation Army Eleven' against a 'German Select Team' played on an asphalt pitch next to a coal mine. We changed on marvellously warm floors and our clothes were attached to trolleys and pulleys and hoisted 30 feet up to the ceiling. After the game our team was shown down the mine but my height meant that I didn't quite fit so I was given a mug of hot cocoa with rum and left on the surface to await their return; we won the match 1–0.

Our last operation in Westphalia was in search of illegal stills; we found nine altogether, six in one morning. None of them produced anything remotely drinkable; one appeared to be the distillate of wood shavings and we actually had to deliver its owner to hospital.

We now received an urgent call to go to Minden and guard the British Admiralty, or 'Admirality' as our several Devonians referred to it. We proceeded at once to that pleasant town taking over a former cavalry barracks, which gave off an unbearable stench due to its occupation down the years by very many horses. It took a great deal of cleaning and hosing down. For no obvious reason the 'Admiralty' had now moved into the town occupying a large white factory building in a middle-class suburb from which 300 families had been evicted from 145 houses at two hours notice. The factory had a vast amount of barbed wire woven round it, mostly by Fred and myself. At 2am one wet and windy morning we were on picket duty, jointly propping up a lamppost. I was enjoying a Mars Bar and Fred had one cigarette glowing away in his mouth and another one unlit behind his right ear, shielded from the rain beneath his beret.

We were still on a war footing so our rifles were loaded and we had been warned against strangers without an appropriate password and especially to look out for 'werewolves' who were very much in vogue at the time. We were not sure who or what they were except that they were said to howl a lot and one was thought to have thrown a grenade at a sentry. Fred had just lit his second cigarette when, from out of nowhere, there appeared a tall, thin ugly man wearing a green beret and carrying a baton which he waved in Fred's face.

'I am a major general,' he declared. 'I am OC Commando Group Europe and I want to inspect your rifle.'

'Ow the 'ell do I know who you are!' Fred replied quite reasonably, 'while we are about it I'm 'Erman bleedin' Goering and just you put yer 'ands well above yer 'ed or I'll shoot yer stone dead!' This would have been Fred's second dead general of the campaign, though his first Allied one. At that moment our new, though only slightly improved, Sergeant Major appeared on the scene.

'Oh, my God,' he said 'do you know who this is Waring?'

'Adolph bleedin' 'itler, as far as I know until he shows me some identification' Fred replied.

'After all Sergeant Major,' I said 'it would be the sentry's responsibility if he did turn out to be Adolph Hitler would it not?'

'Absolute rubbish and stop wasting time,' blustered our senior NCO, but the General interrupted.

'No, no, the man is quite right,' and he took his identification tag from his neck and showed it to Fred who took his time scanning it.

'What's these initials then, them yours sir?' he asked the General, really wasting time now.

'They stand for my religion, I'm a Roman Catholic.'

'I'm a Plymouth Brethren, myself' said Fred handing the tag back.

That should have concluded proceedings and would have done if the General had had enough brains, but he continued to insist on Fred handing his rifle over and he eventually did, adding helpfully. 'Watch out for one up the spout, sir.' Too late the gun went off with a terrific bang. The officer commanding all Commando forces in Europe stood trembling like an unset jelly while the Sergeant Major dived backwards into a holly hedge. When they had finally recovered and departed complete with blood curdling threats and imprecations, Fred looked at me and said, 'cor, I never put my bleeding' fag out.'

Amongst all the admirals, captains and commanders was a whole fleet of jolly Wrens whom we sought to meet at every opportunity. This had often to be via a system of blind dating. I had arranged to meet a Wren one evening at Minden railway station and arrived well ahead of time. I saw my date but not very clearly and manoeuvred around several pillars to gain a better view. This was not a simple matter and was taking quite a long time when I heard an ever so slightly complaining voice from behind one of the pillars.

'You look alright, I'm sure I can't be that bad to look at can I?' She was lovely and I felt thoroughly ashamed.

Upon our return to urban life we were shown a propaganda film about the perils of venereal disease. The commando had not had a lot of time to spend socialising so there had not been much in the way of VD to worry about. The film was extremely graphic and at another time might have been found both horrifying and salutary but to men fresh from battle it had no effect at all and even caused ribald laughter. I am not sure I had heard of venereal disease before and it certainly made me think.

When we first arrived in Germany any form of fraternising and especially walking out with girls was forbidden and military police roamed about breaking up couples wherever they could be found. Eventually this idiocy ceased and normal life resumed, and in any case it was now that I met Hilde and fell in love. She was older than me and I found her calm temperament a welcome change from the volatile and often hostile atmosphere of the past year. We quickly became very close, forming a happy and exciting physical partnership. It was my first such experience, though my early feelings for Nurse James had come close.

I had seldom met girls before I joined up, after which I came across them aplenty but, although kisses were generously exchanged and I would like to have gone a good deal further, I discovered that for that to happen girls insisted on being wooed and for that to take place I needed not to be forever moving about the country, which was not possible. However I read up about the technique I should need if the great day ever came along. I found a woman's magazine in a train with an exciting article written by someone calling herself Aunt Edna who wrote an early form of agony column in a dashing and amusing style not unlike that of the late Arthur Marshall: informative and funny. Aunt Edna was controversial and ahead of her time. I hope that wasn't why she was left on the train.

In the page I came to treasure she had a long piece entitled ' On marriage' which once it had got over lengthy bits about furnishing the home, gate-legged tables and three piece suites, really set my pulse racing. The foundation of all sound marriages was, in Aunt Edna's opinion, formed in bed as a result of a 'joyous getting together' of both boy and girl and not just as a result of solo activity. Both parties were to benefit and both were responsible for seeing that the other did so. Unfortunately on this highly specific issue she failed to explain anything in detail. That was left for the week ahead and I never managed to get hold of that copy of the paper.

I kept Aunt Edna's advice safely inside a copy of *Motor Cycle* magazine, that being a major enthusiasm of mine at the time. In side this magazine was a rather complex article on the internal combustion engine which seemed to depend on periodic and important explosions, on an intricate system of hard work by throttles, pistons, acceleration and brakes of one sort and another, which all worked together to produce, what the magazine called, maximum lift off. It all sounded like a cheerful if frenetic form of sexual activity and when making love with Hilde and finding my side of the fermentation process going too fast (if I may be permitted to mix my chemistry with my physics) I tried hard to remember the logical workings of a motor cycle engine, with its amazing ability to control itself with well judged acceleration towards its final vital explosion. I wondered what sort of reply I would get from Aunt Edna if I phrase my letter of enquiry in those terms. Meanwhile Hilde and I struggled 'joyously on together'.

Life with the Commando went on until at the end of 1945 when it was disbanded. I received a form to fill out from an administrative centre in London on which the main question seemed to be that I should give compassionate reasons why I felt I should not be drafted to the Far East. That was more or less what it said and without much deep thinking I wrote on it 'wife and five children' and was allowed to stay in Germany, whether because of my reply I don't know. Others who tried funny answers were shipped out to Japan; on the other hand several were released from service altogether.

Stay with Hilde I definitely did. She lived several miles away and, unknown to him, I borrowed the Sergeant Major's bicycle each evening, struggling somewhat to return it by 6am the following morning. Her father was a retired monumental mason and her mother an able cook of what little food there was available. I scrounged what I could from our cookhouse to supplement their meagre rations and we dined together on rather thin stew, sauerkraut from a barrel and black acorn coffee. Eventually I obtained proper coffee, soap, tinned food and, on one occasion, nylons from Nutty Slack, still prospering on the black market. One evening, replete with acorn coffee and sauerkraut, I saw a face at the window and then heard a loud banging at the door. I went to investigate and found an angry looking man in German Army uniform on the doorstep. He called for Hilde who went to the door and returned looking alarmed to say, 'It's Hans Helmut, he's back from the Russian front!' Hans Helmut had been Hilde's boyfriend at school, though rather lost sight of since. She tried explaining matters to him but he became intent on throwing a brick in my direction prior to a hostile entry into the house. I fetched my rifle and confronted him just as he let fly with the brick which fell out of the back of his hand, landing harmlessly in a puddle. Hilde's father arrived on the scene and Hans departed. But the next night he came back and I felt the need to severely threaten him with my rifle. When he eventually left it was for good and I never saw him again, but I did wonder if Hilde ever went back to him later.

Sadly Hilde and I did not survive as a couple. For over two years I tried to gain permission for her to come to England but with no success. I lobbied a Member of Parliament who took the issue up in a personal way but got nowhere. I commuted to and from Germany several times but she seemed less interested on each occasion. I heard indirectly that there was a baby and I hurried over once more. I saw the baby; he was two years old and bore no resemblance to me at all. I wondered if Hans had something to do with it. Nothing was explained, nobody would talk to me. I came home for good and got down to starting a career.

Following the Commando's disbandment Fred and I were sent to another Marine unit on occupation duties in northern Germany. This detachment was not a commando and tried to insist we hand over our green berets as finished and done with. On our joint behalf I refused and continued to refuse despite threats of various disciplinary sanctions. They decided to get rid of us to an army commando still functioning in Holland, complete with green berets.

Someone there looked up my service record and once again noticed that an early entry said 'student' and I was given a job as clerk in their headquarters office where my day consisted of typing leave and travel warrants along with their relevant money and food coupon accompaniments. It occurred to me that as Fred and I seemed to be the only people not going on leave that it shouldn't be too difficult to send ourselves away for a well earned break. I put it to Fred and he agreed, so I procured us army pay books to supplement our own, completing the necessary forms authorising the issue of everything needed for a happy leave. Thus Fred went home to England and I disappeared to stay with Hilde. After three weeks we both returned. We found our unit under notice for imminent disbandment, no one appeared to have missed us and almost at once we found ourselves due for demobilisation. So we turned round and travelled back to Portsmouth to the regimental depot where we had assembled more than four years earlier.

It was at the depot that I met Smokey Cuff for the last time. I have often felt that if the *Magnificent Seven* ever needed an immediate replacement they could do no better than consider my one time friend and ally. I don't know why he was called Smokey; he had actually been a deep-sea fisherman. The fish must have been greatly relieved when he joined up. If there were several distinct human layers in our Commando, one of them being that of pirate captain, Smokey would have qualified. He was a natural warrior from the day he joined us when he was told to deliver a despatch to a nearby unit but turned left instead of right and found he had ridden his motorbike at high speed into the centre of an enemy headquarters. Without a second's hesitation he leapt off his bike, producing a copy of the *Daily Express* neatly folded at the racing results, which he handed to an emerging fully armed German officer. Smokey gave a smart salute and as he rode off called out 'Compliments of Field Marshal Montgomery!' He was just out of sight when the first bullets arrive.

From commando service he had joined the SBS (known as the Special Boat Squadron then now the Special Boat Service). They had employed him as an assassin; his job was to execute German generals. He could go as low as colonel but generals were the preferred target. He claimed two generals, shot dead while opening a bottle of wine to go with a picnic lunch in their staff car. Smokey had re-corked the wine.

Before the Rhine crossing in April 1945, Smokey and two jeep loads of SBS raced across Germany in a bid to capture Admiral Doenitz who was about to become Hitler's successor. They arrived in Bremen at the front of the German Admiralty building as Doenitz fled from the back. During the fight with the guards Doenitz managed to get clean away leaving Smokey and his pals to finish off the breakfast he had started as they arrived. Smokey told me these stories while we were waiting for our demob. He also asked me if I would take his regular girlfriend out for the evening as he had double-booked himself elsewhere and he did not want to let her down. He said her name was Genevieve, she was a red haired beauty, and gave me her address in the town.

I found her house one of a long line of very small terraced properties in the naval quarter, and rang the bell. A large comfortable sort of woman came to the door and looked me up and down. I tried to introduce myself but was interrupted by a powerful voice from somewhere at the back of the house.

'Ask him what he wants Mother!'

'I'm just about to dear.'

'Who does he say he is then?'

'He says he's come to take Genevieve out, as Smokey can't.'

'What does he mean, Smokey can't? Who the hell is he?'

'Come and ask him yourself, dear.'

'I certainly will, tell him to hang on.'

'You're to hang on,' concluded Mother. There was a pause, the house began to shake and presently the most enormous man I had ever seen filled the small doorway, six foot four inches I guessed, and about the same wide.

'And who do you think you are? And why ain't Smokey here to take Genevieve out?' I tried without success to satisfy him on both counts. 'Well then, what have you got planned?' I said I thought a visit to the cinema would be nice. 'You're not taking her to the cinema, oh no you're not.'

'Righto!' I said 'how about the repertory theatre followed by afternoon tea?' That was vetoed and then he asked, 'Do you know who I am?' Before I could reply I heard him say 'I'm the heavyweight champion of the Mediterranean Fleet and the Home Fleet before that. You can take her to afternoon tea and have her back by five o'clock, not a minute later.'

I thought: I'm not going ahead with this nonsense, and was on the point of leaving when for the first time Genevieve emerged – green eyes, green dress, long red hair, trim ankles. I cancelled my return travel plans and agreed to the afternoon tea schedule. Alas, Genevieve didn't throw her arms around me and rain kisses on me, although I plied her with jam, scones and any number of chocolate éclairs. She scoffed almost 30 shillings worth, almost £8 in today's money, but hardly said a word. I had her back home I thought at 5pm, though the heavyweight champion waiting, watch in hand, claimed I was two minutes late.

Back at the barracks I searched everywhere for Smokey but he was nowhere to be found and I never saw him again. The next day I left Portsmouth as a civilian. They gave me a marvellous double-breasted pin-striped suit, a pair of shoes in the wrong size, several shirts and for some reason a bowler hat, along with £57. It was rather an anti-climax.

I was sent to an isolation hospital on Hayling Island to recover from a last minute attack of German measles and read the *Boy's Own Paper*, which was all I could find while I lay on my bed considering the last four years. I thought a little but not much about the fighting, I thought not at all of the enemy that were the Germans but remembered our Sergeant Major in some detail including the hand grenade throwing competition I had won to see who could drop one nearest to him, and I recalled the look of surprise on his face. But most of all I thought of the extraordinary young men I had met who became my friends and especially little Fred Waring my best mate, companion and lifesaver. I don't remember feeling any guilt at surviving, though I though of the unlucky ones with respect and affection.

Appendix I

At the end of 1945 the Commando was disbanded. It had suffered a 50 per cent casualty rate on D-Day in killed, wounded or missing, including all five troop commanders. In helping in the liberation of Holland and the freeing of the approaches to Antwerp, a further third of their number became casualties. Several very important people wrote nice letters or said encouraging things on disbandment.

Field Marshal Montgomery wrote to say he wished to testify to the unit's valour and devotion in freeing the continent. The divisional commander wrote that whatever had been done had been done well and said that above all else we were always smiling, which pleased Fred, while the Brigadier sent a note to say he thought we were all a jolly good sheet anchor. Finally, in his address at the dedication service, a bishop referred to us as 'smiling young giants', which pleased Fred even more. Several smiling young giants were then sent out to Burma. Some, older than the others, were returned to civilian life and some stayed on to help out in Germany.

Being a sensitive young giant I felt it hard to shake off the unpleasant memories and surprisingly my nightmares plagued me for years. I never felt a sense of fulfilment or any feeling that I was glad to have been there or wouldn't have missed it for the world as some did. I was really proud to have been accepted as a friend among the quirky, brave and often funny men who formed an elite infantry section at war.

In retrospect I tend to resent the politicians busy disbanding regiments, men who have never been stood on their heads by shock of shell, never been fired upon or been compelled to listen to the despair and resentment of a badly injured comrade.

Appendix II

What did I feel I was fighting for?

Certainly for my survival and that of my immediate pals. For anyone at all who resembled my old friend Walter Summerbee who worked for very little money well into his seventies as a traveller for a brewery company. One day Walter gave me a lift in his car on condition we stopped at the local co-operative cemetery to view his intended funeral plot. At the ornate gates we were welcomed by the official in charge, closely resembling the main supporting character that caused such mayhem in all the Will Hay comedies. Not many teeth, a white, straggly beard and a high querulous voice.

'I'm glad I caught you Walter,' he declared, as we stood contemplating Walter's plot, 'we've a very special offer on at the moment, it's a three for two on hymns, choose an extra one – and you've already booked two – and we give you one free.'

'What's the catch?' asked Walter.

'Well you have to die before the end of the month.'

'I'll see what I can do,' said Walter 'I'd like that extra hymn.' The gatekeeper left us and Walter seemed lost in thought, finally he said, 'I love this spot, just see that view of the hills and all this lovely sunshine. It will catch the sunshine from here!'

'But how will you see it Walter?' I asked.

'Oh, I shan't,' he said, 'but think how nice it will be for my visitors.'

And who did I definitely not fight for?

Those who were present one Hogmanay in the 1950s at Tollcross in Edinburgh who while my car was stuck in traffic, knocked on the window and when it was opened hit me hard in the face, ripped off my wing mirrors, jumped onto the car bonnet and finally kicked in my headlamps. Not that they retired unscathed because, being full of sparking Bordeaux and Dutch courage, I recalled the Commando's unofficial moto 'Maximum surprise followed by maximum violence' and lurched from my car after the miscreants. Instinctively employing the brutal form of unarmed combat I had been taught a long time ago, I laid all three opponents out of action on the pavement and severely damaged their two reinforcements who had come to their rescue. I then ran out of breath but managed to avoid disaster by calling out 'Police, police!' They didn't come, of course, but fortunately the drunken rascals ran off.

The fight finished at a bus stop alongside a bus inspector and several elderly women awaiting a bus who had been cleaning the nearby *Palais de Dance*. There was much clicking of tongues and one old dear said, 'You big 'uns are always picking on yon wee 'uns, you should be ashamed of yourself!'

'I've never seen such violence in my life, I wish I'd called the police,' the bus inspector said. I told him I wished he had too and reminded him that I had actually done so. I pointed to my battered car and asked,

'How's that for violence?'

'You Sassenachs are all the same!' he said. I went home.

Postscript

At London Zoo, in the high summer of 1946, I was in the monkey house with Bobby, my fiancée and her rather fierce aunt, Lady B, who was exercising her rights as a Fellow of the Zoo to have monkeys up to medium size removed from their cage and draped over her shoulder. A parade ground voice from a nearby seat sliced through the pleasantries. 'Wotcher Lofty, up to monkey business are we!' Sergeant Kemp, Military Medal and Member of the Order of the Bronze Lion of the Netherlands, and his pretty wife.

About to catch a train at Marylebone station a week later, I heard a much remembered voice, 'Wor, wor, wor, wor, wotcher Lofty!' Hurling mailbags about was Steve, our virtuoso performer on his Bren gun. One of our two gallant stammerers.

Lastly and best of all, along the Earls Court Road on a blustery November afternoon a dustbin lorry braked sharply, screeched and skidded to a perilous halt on the pavement. Its driver jumped out and, along with two rough looking scamps from the back, ran shouting loud, happy uncomplimentary greetings. Two Bills and a Bert, not seen for nearly a year.

On the sixtieth anniversary of VE Day amongst all the palaces of remembrance on radio and television with parades up and down the Mall and flights of ancient aeroplanes overhead I found myself, bereft of medals or green beret, standing with my two cocker spaniels in the small Lancashire mill town of Barrowford. At precisely eleven o'clock round the bend in the road emerged the town brass band blazing away, ever so slightly off key, a medley of popular wartime tunes and led by a splendid giant veteran hurtling along on a genuine wooden peg leg and blowing like mad on a trombone. The dogs and I joined the service that followed in the market square. There weren't many of us there, 30 or 40 perhaps. Camaraderie in large amounts followed in the British Legion hall together with fine roast beef sandwiches. That was what it so sensibly was all about, simple heartfelt memories and lots of laughter. The sun shone all day.

Index